Fractured Fairy Tales

for

Student ACTORS

A collection of
contemporary
fairy tale scenes

Jan Peterson Ewen

MERIWETHER PUBLISHING LTD.
Colorado Springs, Colorado

Meriwether Publishing Ltd., Publisher
PO Box 7710
Colorado Springs, CO 80933-7710

www.meriwether.com

Editor: Theodore O. Zapel
Assistant editor: Nicole Rutledge
Cover design: Jan Melvin

© Copyright MMXIII Meriwether Publishing Ltd.
Printed in the United States of America
First Edition

Library of Congress Cataloging-in-Publication Data

Ewen, Jan Peterson.
  [Plays. Selections]
  Fractured fairy tales for student actors : a collection of contemporary
fairy tale scenes / by Jan Peterson Ewen. -- First edition.
      pages cm
  ISBN 978-1-56608-192-4 (pbk.)
  1. Fairy tales--Drama. 2. Fairy tales--Adaptations. I. Title.
  PS3555.W46F73 2013
  812'.54--dc23
                                      2012047676

            1   2   3   13   14   15

To the many performers and crew members I have worked with over the years, and especially to my acting students, who have been my extremely supportive guinea pigs. To my mother, who taught me to sing, forced me to take piano lessons, and always put my manuscripts at the top of her reading list. She showed me that creativity is essential to living a happy life, and she was so right. I love you, Mom.

Table of Contents

Introduction

Working with acting students in the creative theatrical process is one of my great joys. Whether participating in a class or main stage production, the personal skills developed through the art of acting open up vast new worlds of opportunity to the student, regardless of age. Yet, as an instructor I have been challenged to find effective, appropriate resources to aid in the learning process. Necessity, being the proverbial "mother of invention," has inspired me to create a series of scenes that fit the needs of my acting students, both children and adults. The scenes have become so popular with my students and have filled such a gap in the material I needed that I began to think they might be a welcome resource for other teachers and directors as well. I like humor. Actually, I love humor. Most often I prefer directing a good comedy over a dramatic piece. Don't get me wrong, there is definitely a place for dramatic work in the process of developing acting skills. But for most students I encounter, comedy is a logical and easy first step into the theatre. Comedy helps loosen up the students' inhibitions and gives them permission to have fun with the learning process. Characterizations become broader and theatrical elements are learned with little effort.

The scenes contained in this book are based on familiar characters with a comedic spin on their situations. I looked at the characters and situations presented in children's rhymes, stories, and songs and took a slightly different approach to the storylines. I have included the reference stories and rhymes that correspond with each scene as, believe it or not, the majority of my young students do not know many of the common nursery rhymes on which the scenes are based.

Most of the characters may be played by either gender, and several scenes can be expanded to accommodate an entire classroom. Each scene explores different theatrical components identical to those found in full-length scripts. For example, several scenes deal with the understanding that something has just occurred Off-stage. The scene then unfolds around the unseen event, affecting the characters as they enter the stage and all the events and reactions that follow. Some scenes are based on specific genres. Some scenes are based on the development of characters and relationships. Some revolve around the discovery of new information and the process of solving problems and finding solutions.

These scenes should not be limited to use by young acting students. My adult and youth acting classes love performing them as well. Through their presentations, my adult actors become very creative, develop colorful characters, and discover the ability to create naturally expressive dialogue.

It is my sincere hope that you and your students will enjoy this material as much as my students have, and that it will add reams of opportunities to your current wealth of resources.

— Jan Peterson Ewen

Scenes for Two to Three Actors

1. Have a Seat

Cast of Characters:
VIRGINIA Muffet, a self-assured young girl.
SPIDER, a boastful bully.

Props:
Bowl, spoon, bottle of Tabasco sauce, and lunchbox

Scene:
Outside Virginia Muffet's school at lunchtime. Place a bench at Center Stage.

1 *(VIRGINIA enters carrying her lunchbox and looks*
2 *around for a suitable place to sit. Upon finding a bench*
3 *she likes, she sits, opens her lunch, and takes out a bowl,*
4 *a spoon, and a bottle of Tabasco sauce. She begins to slurp*
5 *from the bowl with the spoon. A rather sleazy-looking*
6 *SPIDER enters opposite her. SPIDER looks around the*
7 *playground for a victim, spots VIRGINIA, straightens up,*
8 *and saunters over to her casually.)*
9 **SPIDER:** *(Clears throat to get VIRGINIA's attention. She*
10 *doesn't respond. Slyly)* **Boo!** *(VIRGINIA looks up and*
11 *smiles sweetly. SPIDER looks slightly confused at her*
12 *calm reaction but continues on. Pointing to the bench)*
13 **May I have a seat?**
14 **VIRGINIA:** *(Looks up and smiles.)* **Oh, sure.** *(Scoots over to*
15 *make room for SPIDER and then continues enjoying her*
16 *soup. SPIDER is a bit disappointed that his or her initial*
17 *introduction is met with such disregard. SPIDER sits next*
18 *to VIRGINIA, planning his or her next move. After a*
19 *moment, SPIDER turns to VIRGINIA, suddenly making a*
20 *scary face. VIRGINIA just smiles and goes back to eating.*
21 *Once more SPIDER considers her reaction with*
22 *confusion and then turns and makes an even scarier face*

1   *at her. VIRGINIA giggles at these antics. SPIDER stops.)*

2   **SPIDER: What's wrong with you?**

3   **VIRGINIA:** *(Confused)* **Nothing. What's wrong with you?**

4   **SPIDER: You're supposed to be terrified of me and run**

5   **away screaming!**

6   **VIRGINIA: I am? Why would I do that?**

7   **SPIDER: Because ...** *(Points to himself or herself as if*

8   *VIRGINIA should catch on to who SPIDER is.)*

9   **VIRGINIA:** *(Still not recognizing him)* **Because ... why?**

10   **SPIDER:** *(Exasperated)* **Don't you realize who I am?**

11   **VIRGINIA:** *(Scrutinizes SPIDER's face for a moment and*

12   *then gives up.)* **I'm sorry, I don't. Who are you?**

13   **SPIDER: I'm the spider!** *(No reaction from VIRGINIA)* **You**

14   **know** — *the spider!* **You are supposed to run away in**

15   **horror the moment I sit down beside you!**

16   **VIRGINIA:** *(Looks at SPIDER quizzically for a moment and*

17   *then shakes her head.)* **Nope, sorry. Doesn't ring a bell.**

18   **Would you like a pretzel?**

19   **SPIDER: No, I don't want a pretzel! I want to scare you out**

20   **of your wits!**

21   **VIRGINIA: Oh, I see. OK. Well, why don't you try again?**

22   *(Gets herself ready. SPIDER, certain of his or her expert*

23   *skills, makes another full-out attempt at scaring her.*

24   *VIRGINIA lets out a weak little scream.)*

25   **VIRGINIA: Aaaah!** *(Stops.)* **How was that?**

26   **SPIDER: That was pathetic. You obviously didn't mean it.**

27   **VIRGINIA: Really? Well, I'm sorry.** *(Nonchalantly)* **I'm just**

28   **not afraid of spiders.**

29   **SPIDER: Well, you certainly don't have a very good**

30   **attitude about this, missy!**

31   **VIRGINIA: Virginia.** *(Puts her hand out to shake.)* **My name**

32   **is Virginia** — **Virginia Muffet. And you are?**

33   **SPIDER:** *(Disappointed)* **Oh, for heaven's sake. I can't**

34   **believe you still don't know who I am. I'm the famous**

35   **spider who is supposed to scare you right off your**

1   **tuffet! Don't kids read their nursery rhymes**
2   **anymore?**
3   **VIRGINIA: What's a tuffet?**
4   **SPIDER:** *(In disbelief)* **What's a tuffet? You've got to be**
5   **kidding me! It's what you're supposed to be sitting**
6   **on!**
7   **VIRGINIA: How can I sit on a tuffet if I don't even know**
8   **what one is?**
9   **SPIDER:** *(Sighs deeply.)* **OK, let me try to explain. A tuffet**
10   **is a low, padded seat or footstool.**
11 **VIRGINIA:** *(Looks at what she's sitting on.)* **Well, this is a**
12   **bench — not a tuffet.**
13 **SPIDER:** *(Trying to hold it together)* **I can see that this is a**
14   **bench, but it's supposed to be a tuffet so that it**
15   **rhymes with your last name — Muffet. Get it?**
16   *(Comparing the two)* **Tuffet? Muffet?**
17 **VIRGINIA:** *(Giggles.)* **Oh, I get it. That's so cute!**
18 **SPIDER:** *(Rolling his eyes)* **Oh, boy! You see, you are**
19   **supposed to be sitting on a tuffet, eating your curds**
20   **and whey.**
21 **VIRGINIA: Oh, I had curds and whey for breakfast. I**
22   **wanted something a little spicier for lunch, so I'm**
23   **having tortilla soup. Want a taste?** *(Offers SPIDER a*
24   *spoonful.)*
25 **SPIDER:** *(Distracted for a moment by the delicious aroma)*
26   **Mmmm. That does smell good. I love cilantro and**
27   **those little chilis ...** *(Suddenly coming back to his or*
28   *her senses)* **Never mind about the soup! That's close**
29   **enough. At least it's in a bowl. But when I sit down**
30   **next to you, you are supposed to run away in horror.**
31 **VIRGINIA:** *(Considering this)* **But if I run away in horror, I**
32   **might spill my soup, and I am enjoying my soup.**
33 **SPIDER:** *(Thinks a moment. The reasoning approach isn't*
34   *working. SPIDER tries scooting closer to VIRGINIA and*
35   *uses a gruff, scary voice.)* **Aren't you even a little bit**

1   **frightened of me?**
2   **VIRGINIA:** *(Grabs the bottle of Tabasco sauce from her*
3   *lunchbox and holds it up to SPIDER.)* **Look, buddy, I**
4   **have a bottle of Tabasco sauce here, and I am not**
5   **afraid to use it. So back off!**
6   **SPIDER:** *(Slumps down in despair.)* **Oh, what's the use? I**
7   **can't even scare a little girl anymore.** *(Starts to*
8   *whimper.)* **That's the easiest job of all! I am a disgrace**
9   **to arachnids everywhere!**
10   **VIRGINIA:** *(Puts away her lunch and turns to the SPIDER,*
11   *acting as a counselor.)* **It's OK. Let it out. Let it all out.**
12   **There you go. All right, feeling better?**
13   **SPIDER:** *(Sniffles.)* **Maybe a little.**
14   **VIRGINIA: You know, if I may give you my opinion, I think**
15   **you're much too wrapped up in this macho self-image**
16   **you've developed. So you no longer strike fear into**
17   **the hearts of young girls everywhere. Is that the end**
18   **of the world? No, it's not. Maybe it's just time for you**
19   **to reinvent yourself. Turn over a new leaf. Try**
20   **something new. Do you really want people to be**
21   **scared of you all the time? Hmmmm? Do you?**
22   *(SPIDER shakes head "no.")* **Wouldn't you like to have**
23   **a few friends to play with?** *(SPIDER nods "yes.")* **Of**
24   **course you would! So here's what I would like to**
25   **suggest. Go over to that nice, tall waterspout over**
26   **there.** *(Points.)* **And climb up and up, as high as you**
27   **can go. And when you get to the top, I want you to**
28   **shout out to everyone, "I am not a bully!"** *(SPIDER*
29   *looks unsure about this idea. VIRGINIA encourages him*
30   *or her.)* **Go on. Just try saying it first.**
31   **SPIDER:** *(Speaking softly, mumbles.)* **I am not a bully.**
32   **VIRGINIA:** *(In a sing-song manner)* **I can't hear you. Try it**
33   **again with a little more conviction.** *(Shows him or her*
34   *how with a strong voice.)* **"I am not a bully!"**
35   **SPIDER:** *(Gaining confidence)* **I am not a bully!**

1   **VIRGINIA: Wonderful! Now, say it again!**
2   **SPIDER:** *(Stands and says it with gusto.)* **I am *not* a bully! I**
3   **am not a *bully!***
4   **VIRGINIA: Wonderful! You see? Then everyone will know**
5   **what a kind, generous spider you are, and your life**
6   **will be forever changed.**
7   **SPIDER: I can see it! I think you're right! I don't have to**
8   **bully people to feel good about myself. My life can be**
9   **totally turned around. By George, I'm going to climb**
10   **that waterspout and shout it to the world!** *(Practices*
11   *saying it again.)* **I am not a bully!** *(New thought)* **Just**
12   **think, I could be an artist or a poet or someone like**
13   **that. I've always loved knitting.**
14   **VIRGINIA: Hooray!** *(SPIDER marches off triumphantly as*
15   *VIRGINIA calls after him or her.)* **Oh, and Spider, once**
16   **you reach the top of the spout, make sure you keep**
17   **an eye out for rain or you could be in for the ride of**
18   **your life! Good-bye now!** *(Waves good-bye to SPIDER.*
19   *Curtain.)*
20
21
22   **Reference – Nursery Rhyme:**
23   "Little Miss Muffet sat on a tuffet,
24   Eating her curds and whey.
25   Along came a spider and sat down beside her,
26   And frightened Miss Muffet away."
27
28   **Also,**
29   "The itsy-bitsy spider went up the waterspout.
30   Down came the rain and washed the spider out.
31   Up came the sun and dried out all the rain,
32   And the itsy-bitsy spider went up the spout again."

2. Lost and Found

Cast of Characters:

BO PEEP, a girl who tends to lose her sheep.

MARY, a girl who is constantly being followed by her little lamb.

Props:

Box or chair on one side of the stage.

Scene:

An open, outdoor setting.

1 *(BO PEEP enters, searching the stage for the flock of*
2 *sheep she has lost. MARY enters from the opposite side of*
3 *the stage, frantically looking for a place to hide. She*
4 *discovers a box or chair on one side of the stage and*
5 *quickly ducks behind it.)*
6 **BO PEEP:** *(Worried, calling to her sheep)* **Fluffy! Snowball!**
7 **Woolley!** *(Looks around and calls out louder.)* **Here,**
8 **sheep, sheep, sheep!**
9 **MARY:** *(Popping out of her hiding place, speaking in a loud*
10 *stage whisper)* **Shhhh! Can't you see I'm trying to hide**
11 **here? Go away! Go away!** *(Ducks back into her hiding*
12 *place.)*
13 **BO PEEP: Oh, I'm sorry.** *(Looks around the empty stage.)*
14 **Excuse me, who exactly are you hiding from? There's**
15 **no one here but you and me – unfortunately.**
16 **MARY:** *(Pops out again. Pleading)* **Please, just go away. She'll**
17 **be here any minute, I'm sure of it, and I really don't**
18 **want her to find me.** *(Disappears again.)*
19 **BO PEEP: Oh, all right. I'll be gone in a minute, just as soon**
20 **as I find my sheep.** *(Calls again.)* **Here, Snowball! Here,**
21 **Woolley!** *(Whistles.)* **Oh, where have they gone this**
22 **time?**

1   MARY: *(Coming out of hiding once more)* **Shhhh!** *(Begging*
2   *this time)* **Oh, please, could you just go look**
3   **somewhere else for your sheep?** **They're obviously**
4   **not here and your voice will probably be heard by my**
5   **little lamb and, in case you haven't noticed, I am**
6   **trying to hide from her! Now go!**
7   BO PEEP: **Your lamb? What do you mean you're trying to**
8   **hide from her? Why would anyone want to hide from**
9   **their little lamb?**
10   MARY: **It's a long story. Let's just say she follows me**
11   **everywhere I go, and I've had enough of it!**
12   BO PEEP: **Oh, I see.** *(Looks puzzled.)* **No, actually I don't**
13   **see. I've looked everywhere for my flock of sheep,**
14   **and I don't know where to find them. I would give**
15   **anything to see them again.**
16   MARY: **Oh, just leave them alone and they'll come home.**
17   BO PEEP: *(Starts to sniffle. She is noticeably upset.)* **Maybe**
18   **they don't want to come home. Maybe they don't like**
19   **me anymore.**
20   MARY: *(Begins to feel sorry for her.)* **Oh, come now. I'm sure**
21   **they still like you. Do you feed them every day?** *(BO*
22   *PEEP nods "yes" through her tears. With certainty)*
23   **Then they still like you.** *(BO PEEP continues her*
24   *crying. MARY looks uncomfortable and tries to think of*
25   *a way to comfort her. Holding out her hand)* **My name**
26   **is Mary. What's yours?**
27   BO PEEP: *(Through her tears)* **Bo Peep.**
28   MARY: **Bo Peep? Bo Peep? That's your name, really?** *(BO*
29   *PEEP starts to cry louder.)* **OK, OK, I'm sorry. It's a nice**
30   **name; very unique. So look, why don't you tell me**
31   **about your sheep? Maybe I can help. How many are**
32   **missing?** *(BO PEEP still can't talk through her tears.*
33   *She slowly raises four fingers in answer to MARY's*
34   *question.)* **Now we're getting somewhere. Four**
35   **missing sheep.** *(Tries to think of another question to*

1   *ask about them.)* **What are their names?**

2   **BO PEEP:** *(Still sniffling, slowly starts to tell MARY about her*

3   *sheep. She obviously cares for each of them deeply.)*

4   **Well, there's Woolley. He's the oldest and stubborn as**

5   **can be. And there's Snowball, she's the pretty one.**

6   **And Fluffy, he's the ringleader. And last but not least,**

7   **there's Leonard. He's a conformist. Everywhere the**

8   **others go, Leonard is sure to follow.**

9   **MARY: Yeah, sheep will tend to do that. You seem to be**

10   **pretty fond of them. So, how did you lose them?**

11   **BO PEEP: Well, we were out for our daily walk, and I**

12   **stopped to pick a few flowers. When I turned around**

13   **they had taken off, the little rascals. And this is not**

14   **the first time. Yesterday I climbed a tree to pick an**

15   **apple, and when I got down, they were gone.**

16   **Vanished into thin air! The day before that, I was**

17   **looking up at a cloud formation, and when I looked**

18   **back ... Well, you can probably guess.**

19   **MARY: Gone?** *(BO PEEP nods sadly.)* **That's terrible.** *(Trying*

20   *to cheer her up)* **But they've always come home again,**

21   **right?**

22   **BO PEEP: Yes, wagging their stubby little tails behind**

23   **them. But I must admit, it's not just the sheep. I seem**

24   **to lose everything: my cell phone, my iPod, my laptop.**

25   **Why, last week alone I lost my house key, my glasses,**

26   **and my coat all in one day. I'm afraid someday I'm**

27   **going to lose my head!**

28   **MARY:** *(Chuckles.)* **That's funny. I can't seem to lose**

29   **anything, at least when it comes to my sheep.**

30   **BO PEEP: What do you mean?**

31   **MARY: Well, I have this really cute lamb, you see. She's**

32   **adorable and I love her, but I get so frustrated**

33   **because she follows me everywhere I go. To the store,**

34   **to the library, to the park. She even followed me to**

35   **school this morning, which, as you may know, is**

1   against the rules. "No farm animals allowed at
2   school," which I don't really get. I mean, what's the
3   harm if an occasional chicken or pig shows up on the
4   playground? So, I told my lamb to go home, but she
5   just hung around all day on the playground, waiting
6   for me.
7 **BO PEEP:** *(Amazed)* She just waited for you to get done
8   with school? She didn't run away or get lost?
9 **MARY:** Oh, no! She never runs away. And boy, did I get into
10   trouble because of that lamb. My teacher sent me to
11   the principal's office. And worse than that, the other
12   kids laughed at me because I had a lamb at school. It
13   was so embarrassing! So, when school got out, before
14   she could see me, I ran away as fast as I could. *(Looks*
15   *back to see if the lamb has found her yet.)*
16 **BO PEEP:** I wish my sheep would follow me everywhere I
17   go. It would be so much easier.
18 **MARY:** Oh no, you don't! Believe me, it sounds good but
19   it's nothing but a headache.
20 **BO PEEP:** But I think it's so sweet that your little lamb
21   wants to be with you all the time. You're very
22   fortunate.
23 **MARY:** Oh, come on! *(Mimicking the other children)* "Hey,
24   look! There goes Mary with that little lamb following
25   her. Ha, ha, ha!" It's so embarrassing!
26 **BO PEEP:** Well, I think it's sweet and so much easier than
27   chasing your sheep all over the countryside and
28   worrying about them every day like I do.
29 **MARY:** I guess that's true. I never have to chase after her.
30   She's always right beside me and she is awfully cute.
31   *(Imagines her lamb.)* She has a beautiful white fluffy
32   coat.
33 **BO PEEP:** Yes?
34 **MARY:** And cute little ears.
35 **BO PEEP:** How sweet.

1   MARY: And those eyes — I mean, one look into those baby
2   blue eyes, and you melt like butter! *(Starts to sniffle.)*
3   She's so devoted to me. She sleeps at the foot of my
4   bed every night. *(The sniffles turn into full-blown*
5   *tears.)* And when she romps around the yard — it's
6   adorable! *(Crying)* I just love her so much!
7   BO PEEP: *(Comforting MARY)* Of course you do! She's your
8   little lamb. You can't help but love her.
9   MARY: *(Stutters as she dries her tears.)* Maybe I'd better get
10   going. My lamb is probably looking all over for me.
11   She might be scared or worried about me. *(MARY and*
12   *BO PEEP realize they have struck up a friendship.)*
13   BO PEEP: I'd better get going, too. It'll be dark soon, and
14   I've got to find the flock and get them home for their
15   dinner. Thanks for all your help.
16   MARY: It was nothing. Thanks for your help too, Bo Peep!
17   BO PEEP: You're welcome.
18   MARY: *(Starts to leave and then turns back.)* Oh, one more
19   thing to consider — microchips! You might look into
20   getting microchips for your sheep. That way, even if
21   they do roam, you will always get them back again.
22   BO PEEP: *(Considers this.)* Microchips? What a wonderful
23   idea! Why didn't I think of that? I'll call the vet first
24   thing tomorrow morning. Good luck finding your
25   lamb!
26   MARY: Same to you! *(They wave to each other as they exit off*
27   *opposite sides of the stage, calling to their sheep.*
28   *Curtain.)*

1   **Reference — Nursery Rhymes:**

2   "Mary had a little lamb,

3   Whose fleece was white as snow.

4   And everywhere that Mary went,

5   The lamb was sure to go.

6   He followed her to school one day,

7   Which was against the rule.

8   It made the children laugh and play

9   To see a lamb at school."

10

11   **And,**

12   "Little Bo Peep has lost her sheep

13   And doesn't know where to find them.

14   Leave them alone and they'll come home,

15   Dragging their tails behind them."

3. Licking Our Wounds

Cast of Characters:
GREYLAN, the famous wolf from the "Little Red Riding Hood" story.
MARTY, the famous wolf from "The Three Little Pigs" story.
ROSIE, a waitress.

Props:
Sunglasses, pillow, spoon, two forks, order pad, pen, and two menus.

Scene:
Two legendary wolves are meeting for lunch in a diner. They are brothers, and both are sporting injuries. The first wolf, Greylan, has recently had surgery on his gut. The second wolf, Marty, has a tail injury. Place a table and two chairs at Center Stage.

1　*(The scene begins as GREYLAN enters and carefully sits at*
2　*a table for two. He is wearing a pair of sunglasses that he*
3　*lowers to look over from time to time. He is obviously*
4　*hiding from someone or everyone. MARTY enters*
5　*carrying a pillow and walking stiffly. He is wearing an*
6　*overcoat that he keeps close to his body. Each step seems*
7　*to bring him new pain. He crosses to the same table, pulls*
8　*out his chair, places the pillow in just the right spot on the*
9　*chair and slowly lowers himself down.)*
10　**GREYLAN:** *(To MARTY)* **You seem to be moving a little faster**
11　　**today.**
12　**MARTY: Yeah, yeah. It's getting better — slowly but surely.**
13　　**How are you doing?**
14　**GREYLAN: Not bad. Just a little soreness when I laugh.**
15　　**Fortunately, I don't have much to laugh about these**
16　　**days.**

1   **MARTY: I know what you mean. Well, you're looking**
2   **better anyway. Getting that silver color back in your**
3   **cheeks.**
4   **GREYLAN:** *(Perking up, picks up a spoon and uses it as a*
5   *mirror.)* **Do you think so? That's good. I'm really**
6   **trying to get back out there — on the hunt, you know.**
7   **MARTY: Of course I know. What's a wolf without his hunt?**
8   **He might as well be a poodle or a Chihuahua, for**
9   **heaven's sake.** *(Shudders at the thought.)* **We just need**
10   **to be patient, that's all. Injuries like ours don't heal**
11   **overnight.** *(Moves uncomfortably in his chair and*
12   *groans.)*
13   **GREYLAN: No, they certainly do not. These are major**
14   **injuries —** *major!* *(Moves uneasily in his chair, trying to*
15   *get comfortable. Boasts.)* **After all, I had thirty-one**
16   **stitches!**
17   **MARTY: That's nothing! I got third-degree burns over the**
18   **entire lower half of my body! And believe me, it's a**
19   **little embarrassing waiting for the fur to grow back!**
20   *(Draws the long coat around his legs.)*
21   **GREYLAN:** *(Rubbing his stomach)* **I know what you mean!**
22   **What's a wolf without his beautiful fur?**
23   **MARTY: He's nothing, that's what he is! A wolf's thick coat**
24   **is his pride!**
25   **GREYLAN: It's his joy!**
26   **MARTY: It's the key to his terrific good looks.** *(MARTY and*
27   *GREYLAN each pick up a fork from the table and begin*
28   *to comb their hair. Then both squirm uncomfortably in*
29   *their chairs again. ROSIE walks up to their table with*
30   *her order pad and pencil.)*
31   **ROSIE: All right, boys, what's it going to be?**
32   **MARTY:** *(Looking over his menu)* **What are the specials**
33   **today, Rosie?** *(With each new mention of a pork menu*
34   *item, he winces.)*
35   **ROSIE: Well, let's see, we've got pigs in a blanket, ham and**

1   eggs, pork tenderloin, and navy bean soup.

2   **MARTY: Navy bean soup sounds good.**

3   **ROSIE:** *(Finishes.)* **With ham hocks.**

4   **MARTY:** *(Disgusted, throws down his menu.)* **Ham hocks?**

5   **Ugh! Forget it!**

6   **GREYLAN:** *(Looking at his menu)* **And how is the prime rib**

7   **today, Rosie?**

8   **ROSIE: Aged to perfection and served with one of**

9   **Granny's special muffins on the side.**

10 **GREYLAN:** *(Puts down his menu in disgust.)* **I think we're**

11   **going to need another minute or two to think about**

12   **it.**

13 **ROSIE: Suit yourself.** *(Turns and walks off.)*

14 **MARTY: By the way, the newspaper called today. They are**

15   **doing a story called "Recent Wolf Bloopers," and**

16   **asked if I would give them an interview.**

17 **GREYLAN:** *(Shocked)* **An interview? You didn't agree to it,**

18   **did you?**

19 **MARTY: Of course not! I wouldn't give those smart-alecky**

20   **little pigs the satisfaction of seeing my face plastered**

21   **all over the front of the newspaper. So, I told the**

22   **reporter he should go talk to you.**

23 **GREYLAN: Talk to me? Are you crazy? I'm not talking to**

24   **the press! How embarrassing! I can see the story now.**

25   **"Gluttonous wolf caught in the act of consuming**

26   **sweet little old granny and her red-caped**

27   **granddaughter." How humiliating! No, thank you!**

28 **MARTY: If it hadn't been for that nosy hunter who**

29   **happened by, you might have gotten away with it. I**

30   **still don't know how he recognized you dressed as**

31   **Granny. You are a master of disguise!**

32 **GREYLAN: Well, thank you, but it may have been that little**

33   **piece of red fabric dangling from my mouth as I slept**

34   **– though I'm not certain.**

35 **MARTY: You always have been a messy eater. Mother tried**

1   to teach you manners, but you wouldn't listen.

2   GREYLAN: Me? What about you, brother? At least I

3   managed to catch my meal. You never even got close

4   to your prey.

5   MARTY: *(Defensively)* Well, it's not my fault! That last

6   house was built like a rock! My asthma started

7   flaring up, and I just didn't have enough breath left

8   to blow it down. I tried! Heaven knows I tried! I

9   huffed and huffed several times, and I even puffed

10   awhile, but it wouldn't budge.

11   GREYLAN: *(Starts to snicker to himself.)* But sliding down

12   the chimney? Really? *(His laughter grows.)*

13   MARTY: What's so funny about that? It was a brilliant

14   idea!

15   GREYLAN: Oh, really? Brother, you were outsmarted by

16   three little pigs! Three little, itty-bitty, pink pigs! It's

17   hysterical. You climb up the chimney like a crazy-

18   wolf and expect to drop in and surprise your dinner

19   while they were sitting quietly playing cards. Come

20   on! The smoke should have been your first clue that

21   your plan wasn't going to work!

22   MARTY: I didn't see the smoke until it was too late.

23   Anyway, who are you to talk? Running around the

24   countryside with a belly full of stones, howling like a

25   maniac. Like that's dignified. *(Starts to laugh.)* Boy,

26   that Granny was so mad! She got you good!

27   GREYLAN: All right, all right, stop your laughing. I guess

28   neither one of us has much to brag about. Let's just

29   keep it quiet and hope the whole thing blows over.

30   Soon no one will even remember it happened.

31   MARTY: *(Defensively again)* Blows over? Very funny.

32   *(ROSIE approaches the table again.)*

33   ROSIE: OK, boys. Have you made up your minds? What's it

34   going to be?

35   MARTY: Well, definitely not the Pigs in a Blanket.

1   **GREYLAN: And no baked goods either!**

2   **MARTY: I think we're going to go vegetarian for a while,**

3   **Rosie. We'll have two orders of pasta primavera, if**

4   **you don't mind.**

5   **GREYLAN: And *no* aged cheese on top!**

6   **ROSIE: Right. Two orders of pasta primavera. Hold the**

7   **sausage. Hold the parmesan. Can I get you fellows**

8   **anything else?**

9   **GREYLAN: Not unless you can get us our dignities back!**

10   *(ROSIE exits as MARTY and GREYLAN squirm in their*

11   *chairs, moaning in pain. Curtain.)*

12

13

14   **Reference — Fairy Tales:**

15   The Story of "The Three Little Pigs"

16   The Story of "Little Red Riding Hood"

4. We're Not Just Good-Lookin'

Cast of Characters:
SAM, the pig brother who built the straw house.
GEORGE, the pig brother who built the stick house.
JOE, the pig brother who built the brick house.

Props:
Door and logs to build fire.

Scene:
Inside the brick house that Joe has built.

1   *(As the scene begins, JOE is frantically pulling his*
2   *frightened brothers, GEORGE and SAM, into his house*
3   *through the front door.)*
4   **JOE: Hurry! Hurry! Get in here so I can lock the door!** *(SAM,*
5   *GEORGE, and JOE manage to get the door locked behind*
6   *them. Then, with their backs pressed against the door,*
7   *they all breathe heavily as they catch their breath. JOE*
8   *recovers first.)* **Well, you two take the cake! You could**
9   **have been killed!**
10 **GEORGE: It wasn't my fault. It was Sam!** *(Points to SAM.)*
11 **SAM: You can't blame me for this! I didn't do anything**
12   **wrong!** *(SAM and GEORGE start to fight, simultaneously*
13   *arguing with lines such as, "Why, you!" "You can't talk to*
14   *me like that." "I oughta knock your block off!" "Take that*
15   *back!")*
16 **JOE:** *(Pushes his way between them.)* **All right you two, break**
17   **it up. Break it up! You're both a couple of blockheads!**
18 **SAM: What are you talking about? We're not blockheads! We**
19   **did exactly what you told us to do.**
20 **GEORGE: Yeah! We did exactly what you told us to do. We**
21   **each built a house so we could live out on our own.**

1   SAM: Yeah! We were out in the world, living on our own
2   and having the time of our lives!
3   JOE: Yeah? Well, how did that work out for you? You put up
4   your houses as fast as you could so you could go off
5   and party with your friends. Well, where are those
6   friends now, huh? Why didn't you run to them when
7   you got into trouble?
8   GEORGE and SAM: *(Embarrassed Ad-lib)* Well, uh ...
9   JOE: And what about those houses you built? Did they
10   protect you? *No!* *(SAM and GEORGE look sheepish.)*
11   There's nothing left but a pile of straw and a stack of
12   sticks. Blockheads!
13   GEORGE: *(Defensively)* You told us to go build houses for
14   ourselves. You didn't say what kind of houses.
15   SAM: Yes! I was being thrifty and earth-conscious. Haven't
16   you heard of global warming? Straw is a sustainable
17   material and very eco-friendly. How did I know a wolf
18   could blow it apart in one puff? There was no
19   warning on the recyclable packaging!
20   JOE: You mean it never occurred to you that a straw house
21   might not be particularly strong against the
22   elements? The wolf blew it down in one puff. Just
23   imagine what a little rain or a windstorm might have
24   done! *(GEORGE begins to laugh at SAM for getting into*
25   *trouble. JOE turns to GEORGE.)* And you! *(GEORGE*
26   *runs behind SAM and cowers.)* Remember how I
27   always told you to measure twice and cut once?
28   GEORGE: That sounds vaguely familiar.
29   JOE: Well, did you even measure once? You always rush
30   through your jobs. You never take enough time to see
31   that the job's done right. And look what happened!
32   All you have left is a pile of kindling. A good wood-
33   frame structure takes time and know-how. Did you
34   have any idea what you were doing? Did you read up
35   on it at all?

1　GEORGE: Well ... not really. I thought I could just figure it
2　　　out by myself.
3　JOE: Oh, sure! So, here we are again – you two in hot water
4　　　and me bailing you out. What am I going to do with
5　　　you? *(There is a tense pause.)*
6　SAM: I know! Why don't you make us a cup of tea and
7　　　some muffins? I'm starving!
8　GEORGE: Me, too. Do you have any scones? I just adore a
9　　　nice scone with my tea!
10　JOE: *(Throwing his hands up in frustration)* I don't believe
11　　　you two! Don't you understand that we still have
12　　　work to do? Your stomachs will just have to wait.
13　SAM: What do you mean? We're safe now. There's no way
14　　　the Big Bad Wolf can get into your brick house, Joe.
15　　　You're a master builder.
16　GEORGE: That's right, Joe. You built your house with the
17　　　strongest materials available. We can rest safely here.
18　　　There's no way the Big Bad Wolf will ever huff and
19　　　puff this place down. How about a game of cards?
20　SAM: That sounds wonderful! Let's play Hearts.
21　JOE: No, no, no! Don't you see? That wolf may not be able
22　　　to blow my house down, but he's crafty! He won't stop
23　　　at huffing and puffing! He'll look for another way to
24　　　get in, and then where will we go? We have no more
25　　　brothers to run to! We must think about this
26　　　carefully. Consider the possibilities. *(They begin to*
27　　　*pace as they think.)*
28　GEORGE: Well, he can't climb in the windows – they're
29　　　boarded shut! *(More pacing)*
30　SAM: And he can't get in through the door – we locked it
31　　　tight! *(They pace some more.)*
32　GEORGE: *(Stops suddenly.)* I say we're safe!
33　SAM: Me, too!
34　GEORGE: Now, let's play cards and have some tea and
35　　　scones.

1   SAM: George and I will get the water boiling.
2   JOE: *(Finally stops pacing. He has a realization.)* **That's it!**
3   **Why, I declare, you two are brilliant!**
4   GEORGE and SAM: *(They stop. Suspiciously, together)* **We**
5   **are?**
6   JOE: **Yes! The only way the wolf can get into this house is**
7   **to climb up to the roof and slide down the chimney! If**
8   **you heat up water in the fireplace, the wolf will scald**
9   **himself when he reaches the pot and fly back up to**
10 **the roof in a panic! What a brilliant idea!**
11 GEORGE and SAM: *(Together)* **It was?**
12 JOE: **Oh, brothers, I am so sorry I ever doubted you. You**
13 **have saved us!**
14 GEORGE and SAM: *(Together)* **We have?**
15 JOE: **Come on. I'll help you build up the fire.** *(Stops, puts*
16 *his arms around his brothers' shoulders, and says*
17 *proudly)* **What a team we are. The three Pig brothers!**
18 **No one messes with us, right?** *(Hugs them again.)*
19 **We're not just good-lookin'. We're smart, too!**
20 GEORGE and SAM: *(Still not sure what they did to help.*
21 *Together)* **Right!** *(They shrug and then run to help JOE*
22 *build the fire. Curtain.)*
23
24
25 **Reference — Fairy Tale:**
26 The Story of "The Three Little Pigs"

5. Cheer Up, Cat

Cast of Characters:

COW, an aspiring moon-jumper.

CAT, a famous fiddler.

LITTLE DOG, an easily-amused canine.

Props:

Bench set at Center Stage.

Scene:

An exterior, park-like setting.

1   *(CAT is sitting alone on a bench. He looks glum. COW*
2   *enters in a huff. She is very upset about something that*
3   *has just happened Off-stage.)*
4   **COW:** *(On a mission. She looks for CAT as she enters.)* **Cat? Cat!**
5   **Oh, there you are. I need your help, Cat! You have got to**
6   **do something about Little Dog. He is driving me crazy!**
7   **CAT:** *(Very depressed. Doesn't look up as he talks to COW.)* **Oh.**
8   **Hi, Cow.**
9   **COW: Cat? Did you hear me? You have to do something about**
10   **Little Dog. He won't listen to me, and it's got to stop!**
11   **CAT: What is it, Cow?** *(Hysterical laughter is heard Off-stage.)*
12   **COW: Do you see what I mean? It's terrible, and he won't**
13   **stop laughing!** *(LITTLE DOG enters, holding his sides*
14   *and laughing loudly. He points at COW who stands with*
15   *hands on hips, scowling at him. CAT slowly looks up at*
16   *them. It is obvious that he doesn't care about their*
17   *argument.)*
18   **LITTLE DOG:** *(Can barely talk.)* **Oh, Cat, you've got to come**
19   **watch this with me. It's hysterical. She's doing Zumba**
20   **and yoga, running laps, and practicing her splits.**
21   *(Imitates COW's activities.)* **It's the funniest thing I've**
22   **ever seen!**

1 COW: I'm in training, Little Dog, and I will not let you or
2   anyone else discourage me from reaching my goals.
3   Now, go find something useful to do and leave me
4   alone. I've got to be in top shape for tonight.
5 LITTLE DOG: *(Laughing again)* Did you hear that, Cat? Do
6   you know what she's training for? Moon-jumping!
7   Moon-jumping! It's so ridiculous. Who ever heard of a
8   cow jumping over the moon? It's not natural! I have
9   one word for you, Cat — gravity! Am I right?
10 CAT: *(Sadly)* Right, Little Dog, gravity. But why don't you
11   let Cow get back to her training? Find something else
12   to do. *(LITTLE DOG and COW look at each other,*
13   *forgetting their own argument for the time being. They*
14   *are now concerned about CAT's sadness.)*
15 COW: Cat? Cat, what's wrong? You look so sad. Has
16   something happened?
17 LITTLE DOG: You can tell us, Cat. We're your friends.
18   Maybe we can help. *(CAT looks up at them sadly. COW*
19   *and LITTLE DOG sit on either side of CAT.)*
20 CAT: Oh, thanks. You're such good friends. But there's
21   really nothing you can do to help. It's too late.
22 COW: Too late for what, Cat? Did something happen to
23   your fiddle?
24 CAT: No. It's not my fiddle.
25 LITTLE DOG: Didn't you get your usual dish of warm milk
26   for breakfast?
27 CAT: Oh! *(Starts to cry out loud. LITTLE DOG has apparently*
28   *hit a nerve.)*
29 COW: Oh, dear! Was the milk sour? I can get some fresh for
30   you if you like.
31 CAT: No, I'm sorry. It's not the milk. *(Sniffles.)* It's Dish.
32 LITTLE DOG: Dish? What happened to Dish? *(Expecting*
33   *the worse)* Did she ... break?
34 CAT: *(Stands and breaks away from them.)* No, no. I'm sorry.
35   Don't worry, I'll get over it. *(Sniffling some more)* It's

1   not important.
2 COW: Not important? Cat, if something is upsetting you
3   this much, it must be important. Please tell us about
4   it. *(CAT sits down again.)*
5 CAT: Well, you remember last night at the party?
6 LITTLE DOG and COW: *(Ad-lib)* Oh, yes. It was a wonderful
7   party!
8 CAT: I was playing my fiddle and everyone was dancing
9   and laughing.
10 LITTLE DOG: I could have danced all night!
11 CAT: Well, while we were all having fun at the party,
12   something terrible happened!
13 LITTLE DOG and COW: *(Ad-lib)* Oh, no! What happened?
14 CAT: *(Gathers his strength and speaks slowly and*
15   *deliberately.)* Dish ...
16 LITTLE DOG and COW: *(Together, urging CAT to tell more)*
17   Dish ...
18 CAT: Ran away ...
19 LITTLE DOG and COW: *(Together, urging CAT to tell even*
20   *more)* Dish ran away ...
21 CAT: *(Finally spills it.)* With Spoon!
22 COW: No!
23 LITTLE DOG: I don't believe it!
24 COW: Dish ran away with Spoon? Oh, my. No wonder
25   you're so upset!
26 CAT: Yes. My very own little Dish! Running away with that
27   delinquent, Spoon! He's always getting into hot water
28   and stirring things up. Dish is so fragile! And Spoon
29   is practically unbreakable. I'm so worried about her.
30   *(Sniffs.)* She didn't even say good-bye.
31 LITTLE DOG: *(Trying to see the bright side)* I'm so sorry,
32   Cat. But, you know, they do have quite a bit in
33   common. They both come from the china cabinet.
34 COW: That's true, Cat. And they both work in the food
35   service industry.

1   **CAT:** *(Still sniffling)* **You're right. They do have a lot in**
2   **common. I just hope she'll be OK. Oh, I'm just going**
3   **to miss her so much!**
4   **COW:** *(Comforting CAT)* **We know, Cat. But she may come**
5   **back.**
6   **LITTLE DOG: That's right, Cat. She may come back and**
7   **serve your milk again. We'll just have to wait and see.**
8   **In the meantime, I've got something that will cheer**
9   **you up! Let's go watch Cow work out. It's a hoot!**
10   *(Starts to laugh at the thought.)*
11   **COW: Oh, Little Dog! You'll never stop, will you? Come on,**
12   **Cat. Let's go stare at the beautiful moon for awhile.**
13   **By the way, can you play Zumba music on that fiddle**
14   **of yours?** *(ALL exit together. Curtain.)*
15
16
17   **Reference — Nursery Rhyme:**
18   "Hey, diddle diddle, the cat and the fiddle,
19   The cow jumped over the moon.
20   The little dog laughed to see such sport
21   And the dish ran away with the spoon."

6. Is the Doctor In?

Characters:

JILL, a girl who has recently tumbled down a steep hill.

JACK, a boy who has tumbled down the same hill, hitting his head very hard in the process.

NURSE, the nice lady in the doctor's waiting room.

Props:

Desk, two chairs, and a glass of water.

Scene:

A doctor's waiting room. There is a desk and two chairs in the room. Jack and Jill have just endured a hazardous fall down a steep hill. Jill is seeking medical attention for Jack, whom she thinks may have suffered a serious head injury.

1　*(As the scene opens, JILL is carefully leading JACK into*
2　*the waiting room. JACK appears to be dazed. He staggers*
3　*slightly as he walks. He looks confused.)*
4　**JILL:** *(To NURSE)* **Is the doctor in? We need some help.**
5　*(NURSE goes to help JILL support the ailing JACK.)*
6　**NURSE: Oh, dear! What has happened to you?**
7　**JILL: We had a little accident. Come on, Jack, just a little**
8　　　**farther.**
9　**JACK:** *(Confused)* **Is it time for dinner, Mommy?** *(NURSE*
10　*prepares a chair for JACK.)*
11　**NURSE: Right here, young man. Have a seat. There you go.**
12　**JACK:** *(Sits.)* **Thank you, sir. Is the movie about to start?**
13　**JILL:** *(As if talking to a very young child)* **No, Jack. This is the**
14　　　**nurse. We are at the doctor's office. You took a fall**
15　　　**when we climbed the hill to fetch a bucket of water.**
16　　　**Don't you remember?**
17　**JACK: Of course I like September. It's one of my favorite**
18　　　**seasons.**

1   JILL: *(To NURSE)* **You see? He's been like this ever since he**
2   **hit his head.**
3   JACK: **Yes, I think I would like to go to bed.** *(Starts to curl up*
4   *on the chair.)*
5   NURSE: **No, no, Jack.** *(Sets JACK upright in the chair again.)*
6   **You can't go to sleep right now. The doctor will be**
7   **here in just a minute to check you out. Until then**
8   **we'll just stay awake and talk, OK?**
9   JACK: **OK. You're a nice lady.**
10 NURSE: **Well, thank you, Jack. I think you're nice, too.**
11   **Would you like a glass of water?**
12 JACK: **No, thanks. But you know what I would like?**
13 NURSE: **What?**
14 JACK: **A glass of water.**
15 NURSE: **Oh, all right. I'll get you one. You stay right here.**
16   **Don't move, OK?**
17 JACK: **OK, nice lady.** *(NURSE starts for her desk to get a glass*
18   *of water for JACK. JILL follows her. During the following*
19   *conversation, JACK gets up and starts to wander around*
20   *the room in a fog, unseen by JILL and NURSE.)*
21 JILL: **Well, what do you think? Is he going to be all right?**
22 NURSE: **We'll have to see what the doctor says. That must**
23   **have been quite a fall. He seems very confused. What**
24   **happened exactly?**
25 JILL: **Well, you see, Jack was supposed to give his dog a**
26   **bath today, and I agreed to help him. Bad idea! We got**
27   **a bucket from his mom and headed up to the well to**
28   **fill it. It was going to take two of us to carry it back**
29   **down when it was full of water. So we climbed up that**
30   **steep hill to the well, and believe me, that trail is**
31   **treacherous!**
32 NURSE: **I know what you mean! I've come close to falling**
33   **there myself on several occasions!**
34 JILL: **The town really ought to do something to make it**
35   **safer.**

1   NURSE: I completely agree.

2   JILL: Anyway, Jack isn't the most graceful guy I know —

3   even on a good day. *(JILL and the NURSE finally notice*

4   *that JACK has gotten up and is wandering around. They*

5   *chase after him.)*

6   NURSE: Come back here, Jack! Here's your water. Let's sit

7   down again, all right? *(Leads him back to the chair and*

8   *hands him the glass.)*

9   JACK: Oh, thank you, Grandmother. *(Sits down.)* But I

10   thought I asked for milk.

11 JILL: No, Jack, you asked for water, and this is not your

12   grandmother. It's still the nurse, the "nice lady,"

13   remember? And I'm your friend, Jill. Do you

14   remember falling down the hill?

15 JACK: Do I remember calling Uncle Bill?

16 JILL: Oh, boy!

17 NURSE: Jack, can you tell me what day it is?

18 JACK: Of course I can. It's my birthday! Can I open my

19   presents now, Daddy?

20 JILL: No, Jack. It's not your birthday. There are no

21   presents.

22 JACK: *(Looks sad.)* Oh. Is there cake?

23 JILL: Sorry. No cake either.

24 JACK: You two certainly don't throw a very good birthday

25   party.

26 NURSE: We had better walk him around some more.

27   *(NURSE and JILL pull JACK to his feet and with one*

28   *supporting him on either side they walk him around*

29   *the room as they talk.)* So, how did Jack end up falling

30   down the hill? Did he slip on something?

31 JILL: Not exactly. We reached the top of the hill and

32   started to dip the bucket when a little garter snake ...

33   *(Upon hearing JILL speak the word "snake," JACK*

34   *jumps into the air, letting out a little scream.)* Well, it

35   slithered out from behind the well, and I think you

1   can guess how he lost his footing. Jack is deathly
2   afraid of snakes. *(Upon hearing JILL speak the word*
3   *"snake" again, JACK jumps into the air again and lets*
4   *out a bigger scream.)*
5   JACK: Snake?! Where? Where? *Ahhhh!*
6   JILL: *(To NURSE)* See what I mean? *(To JACK)* Settle down,
7   Jack. You're safe now. There are no snakes here. *(Once*
8   *again, JACK screams. This time he runs to the chair and*
9   *steps up on to it.)*
10 NURSE: It's OK, Jack. I promise. There are no —
11 JILL: *(Stopping the NURSE)* Shhhh! Don't say it!
12 NURSE: *(Carefully choosing her words)* There are no
13   reptiles or any other nasty creatures in this room.
14   Now, just come down from there and relax a bit. The
15   doctor will be ready any minute. *(JACK cautiously*
16   *steps off the chair and sits, looking around the floor,*
17   *just to be sure.)*
18 JILL: Anyway, that's how he fell down the hill. He screamed,
19   completely lost his balance, and the next thing I knew,
20   we were both rolling down the hill at top speed! Jack
21   hit his head on a couple of rocks on the way down, and
22   I came tumbling after him. What a day!
23 JACK: *(Hearing JILL incorrectly)* Where's the sleigh? Is
24   Santa here? I want to see Santa!
25 JILL: Oh, boy! *(NURSE and JILL stand JACK back up again*
26   *and start to walk him Off-stage to the unseen doctor's*
27   *office as they try to quiet his delusions.)*
28 NURSE: Yes, Jack, Santa is here! He is right in the
29   examination room, and he's going to take a look at
30   that bump on your head. Isn't that nice?
31 JACK: Santa's so nice. Are there elves in the examination
32   room, too?
33 JILL: Oh yes, lots of little elves just waiting to take your
34   blood pressure!
35 JACK: And give me presents?

1   **JILL: Oh yes, lots and lots of presents.**
2   **JACK: After all, it's my birthday, you know.** *(ALL exit*
3   *together. Curtain.)*
4
5
6   **Reference — Nursery Rhyme**
7   "Jack and Jill went up the hill
8   To fetch a pail of water.
9   Jack fell down and broke his crown
10 And Jill came tumbling after."

7. Go for the Gold

Cast of Characters:
SPORTY MORTY, from ESPN sports TV.
JACK, of Jack-Be-Nimble "candlestick" fame.

Props:
Microphone.

Scene:
An outdoor track where Jack does his training.

1   *(SPORTY MORTY, talking into a microphone and*
2   *speaking to an unseen TV camera, is On-stage with JACK,*
3   *who is doing some major stretching for his event.)*
4 **SPORTY MORTY: Welcome, sports fans! ESPN's own Sporty**
5   **Morty coming to you live from the Sunshine Stadium**
6   **in Cucamonga, California on this beautiful spring day.**
7   **We are here for an exclusive interview with five-time**
8   **National Candlestick Jumper, Jack Kirkpatrick.** *(JACK*
9   *looks up from his stretching and waves to the imaginary*
10   *camera.)* **We are here today because Mr. Kirkpatrick is**
11   **advocating that his sport, candlestick jumping, be**
12   **accepted into the upcoming Summer Olympics of**
13   **_____.** *(Insert year of next Summer Olympics.)* **Mr.**
14   **Kirkpatrick, may we have a word, please?**
15 **JACK:** *(Stops his warm-up.)* **Please, call me Jack.**
16 **SPORTY MORTY: All right, Jack. Can you please tell the**
17   **folks at home why you feel so strongly that candlestick**
18   **jumping should be added to the roster of the Summer**
19   **Olympics?**
20 **JACK: Well, it's like this, Morty. The Olympics are dedicated**
21   **to featuring the finest athletes and most thrilling**
22   **competitions in the world, and there are no finer**
23   **athletes than candlestick jumpers! This sport takes**

1   skill, daring, flexibility, strength, and years of
2   intensive training.
3 SPORTY MORTY: I see. Candlestick jumping is currently
4   considered an extreme sport. Do you agree with that
5   description?
6 JACK: If you mean "extremely exciting," then absolutely!
7   There is an element of danger to the sport, but look
8   at the extreme sports that have made it into the
9   Olympics in recent years, like snowboarding. Where
10   was snowboarding twenty years ago?
11 SPORTY MORTY: Good point. So how does candlestick
12   jumping compare to the other jumping events, such
13   as the long jump or pole vaulting?
14 JACK: The long jump is more of a horizontal event where
15   the length of the jump is key. Pole vaulting is similar
16   in that it's a vertical jump but, come on, they get to
17   use a long pole to help them get over the beam.
18   Candlestick jumpers do it all on their own, Morty.
19   One vertical leap into the air, clearing the giant taper
20   and flickering flame, landing firmly on the other
21   side. When done by a champion, it's a thing of beauty.
22 SPORTY MORTY: Can you share with the folks at home
23   the training regimen that goes into being a world-
24   class candlestick jumper?
25 JACK: Sure, and this is one of the great things about the
26   sport: it doesn't require a lot of expensive
27   equipment, and you can easily start with items you
28   find at home. In the first stage of training, you learn
29   to jump over birthday candles — *unlit,* of course.
30   Multicolored spirals are best.
31 SPORTY MORTY: Of course.
32 JACK: At this stage, you're perfecting your form and
33   building your stamina. Next, you move on to tea
34   lights, votives. Then the four-inch emergency
35   candles. Once you've mastered your form on the

1   unlit wax, it's time to tackle the big boys — the tapers.
2   SPORTY MORTY: The tapers?
3   JACK: That's right, Morty, the tapers. Now, when it comes
4   to tapers, you've got your six-inch, your ten-inch and
5   finally, your competition standard, the twelve-inch.
6   But remember, twelve-inch candles are for
7   competition *only!* Do not try the twelve-inch tapers at
8   home! You could get seriously burned in all the
9   wrong places! I repeat, the twelve-inch tapers are for
10   competition *only!*
11   SPORTY MORTY: That's an important disclaimer. Do you
12   need any additional equipment to get started?
13   JACK: Well, you will need a good set of sneakers, fire-
14   resistant shorts, and a fire extinguisher, just in case.
15   Better safe than sorry, you know what I mean?
16   SPORTY MORTY: Absolutely! Have many of the athletes
17   been singed during competitions?
18   JACK: Not many. You don't get to this level of competition
19   unless you're safely clearing the flame. But one small
20   slip, and *"Ahhhh!"* (*Lets out a painful scream as if*
21   *recalling an incident.*)
22   SPORTY MORTY: (*Shudders at the thought.*) Well, Jack, you
23   make a good case for adding candlestick jumping to
24   the Olympic schedule. Any last words to our viewers?
25   JACK: I just want to say that this is only the first step in our
26   promotion of candlestick jumping. (*Getting more and*
27   *more excited*) Soon we'll have our logo, "Got flame?"
28   on T-shirts and water bottles. We'll have summer
29   training camps for kids around the world, an
30   international website for support and information, a
31   giant candlestick statue in Central Park, and bumper
32   stickers — lots and lots of bumper stickers!
33   Candlestick jumping will be the next great
34   international sport! You'll see!
35   SPORTY MORTY: Well, thank you very much, Jack. We'll

1   **just have to wait to see how the rest of this story**
2   **develops. Good luck to you, Jack.** *(Addressing the folks*
3   *at home)* **Stay tuned for our report on even more**
4   **extreme sports, including an ambitious cow's**
5   **attempt to jump over the moon! This is Sporty Morty**
6   **signing off.**
7 **JACK:** *(Continuing his last speech toward the camera)* **And**
8   **we'll have a theme song and training DVDs and**
9   **sports camps for beginning candlestick jumpers and**
10   **a complete line of jumping shoes and fireproof**
11   **shorts!** *(Curtain.)*
12
13
14 **Reference – Nursery Rhyme:**
15 "Jack be nimble,
16 Jack be quick.
17 Jack jumped over the candlestick."

8. The Case of the Bitter Butter

Cast of Characters:
TERRY TOOTER, manager of the Better Batter Bakery.
PENNY PIPER, a world-famous detective.

Props:
Notebook and pencil.

Scene:
The scene takes place at the Better Batter Bakery.

1   *(Manager TERRY TOOTER, is pacing nervously back and*
2   *forth, obviously upset. Detective PENNY PIPER enters.)*
3   **PENNY PIPER: I am Detective Penny Piper. I came as swiftly**
4   **as I could.**
5   **TERRY TOOTER:** *(Stops pacing.)* **Thank goodness! Welcome,**
6   **Detective Piper. My name is Terry Tooter. I am the**
7   **manager of the Better Batter Bakery. Thank you for**
8   **coming on such short notice.**
9   **PENNY PIPER: I got your message and came right over.**
10   **What's the emergency?**
11   **TERRY TOOTER: A serious problem has developed here at**
12   **the Better Batter Bakery, and we need your expert**
13   **advice. I am hoping that a famous detective such as you**
14   **can crack the case wide open.**
15   **PENNY PIPER: I will certainly do my best, although I must**
16   **warn you, I am allergic to flour. So pardon me if I start**
17   **to cough or sneeze in your bakery. Now, what seems to**
18   **be the problem?**
19   **TERRY TOOTER: Well, you see, Detective Piper ...**
20   **PENNY PIPER: You may call me Penny.**
21   **TERRY TOOTER: Penny Piper?** *(Stops.)* **Are you, by any**

1   chance, related to Peter Piper?

2   **PENNY PIPER:** *(Sighing)* **Oh, boy, here we go again! Do you**

3   **mean the Peter Piper who picked the peck of pickled**

4   **peppers?**

5   **TERRY TOOTER: Yes, that Peter Piper.**

6   **PENNY PIPER: Unfortunately, I am. Peter Piper is my**

7   **cousin.**

8   **TERRY TOOTER: Really? How fascinating! You know, I've**

9   **always wondered exactly how many pickled peppers**

10   **Peter Piper picked.**

11   **PENNY PIPER:** *(Annoyed)* **Everyone seems to be fascinated**

12   **with Peter Piper and his picked peck of pickled**

13   **peppers. I cannot tell you exactly how many pickled**

14   **peppers Peter Piper picked. As many as it took him to**

15   **fill a peck, I suppose. It's not like it was a world**

16   **record or anything! Now, can we get back to the**

17   **trouble at the bakery?** *(Takes out a notebook and*

18   *pencil and starts to take notes.)*

19   **TERRY TOOTER:** *(Refocusing on the task at hand)* **Oh, yes,**

20   **of course, the trouble at the Better Batter Bakery.**

21   **Well, you see, it all started when one of our best**

22   **bakers, Betty Botter, put some bitter butter into the**

23   **bakery batter.**

24   **PENNY PIPER:** *(Writing this down)* **Bitter butter, you say?**

25   **TERRY TOOTER: Exactly, bitter butter.** *(Explains further.)*

26   **You see, it's not like Betty Botter to put anything but**

27   **the best butter into the bakery batter.**

28   **PENNY PIPER: It's not?**

29   **TERRY TOOTER: Absolutely not!**

30   **PENNY PIPER: So, what happened when Betty Botter put**

31   **the bitter butter into the batter?**

32   **TERRY TOOTER: Well, it turned the batter bitter!**

33   **PENNY PIPER: Oh dear, what a catastrophe for the Better**

34   **Batter Bakery — bitter batter!**

35   **TERRY TOOTER: And that's not the end of it. Because of**

1   the bitter batter, the crusts got crisp, and crisp crusts
2   crackle and crunch, you see?
3   PENNY PIPER: I see. How dreadful. *(Writes in her*
4   *notebook.)* "Crisp crusts crackle and crunch." Go on.
5   TERRY TOOTER: And some of the bitter butter even got
6   into a box of mixed biscuits.
7   PENNY PIPER: A mixed biscuit box?
8   TERRY TOOTER: That is correct. A box of mixed biscuits.
9   A mixed biscuit box.
10   PENNY PIPER: Curious. *(Writes this down.)*
11   TERRY TOOTER: So, Betty Botter had to stop the batter
12   production, go to the grocery store, get some better
13   butter to put in the batter and we had to throw out all
14   the mixed biscuits and the crisp crusts. I haven't seen
15   anything like it since Sally Sutton worked here seven
16   years ago.
17   PENNY PIPER: Sally Sutton? I knew a Sally Sutton. Doesn't
18   she sell seashells down by the seashore?
19   TERRY TOOTER: She does now. Sally couldn't handle the
20   pressure and noise of the bakery business. Any noise
21   annoyed her, but the noisy noise annoyed her more.
22   PENNY PIPER: I see. Very interesting. *(Jots this down in her*
23   *notebook.)* "Annoyed by noisy noise."
24   TERRY TOOTER: It's too bad, really. She made good
25   cookies, and you must know that a good cook can
26   cook as many cookies as a good cook who could cook
27   cookies.
28   PENNY PIPER: Undoubtedly. So, was there anyone else at
29   the bakery on the day the bitter butter showed up in
30   the batter?
31   TERRY TOOTER: Well, there was me — Terry Tooter.
32   *(Watches as she writes down his name.)*
33   PENNY PIPER: *(As she writes)* Terry ... Tooter. *(Looks up.)*
34   You know, I once knew a tutor who tooted the flute.
35   He tried to tutor two tooters to toot. But the two asked

1　the tutor, "Is it harder to toot, or to tutor two tooters
2　to toot?"
3　TERRY TOOTER: That's a very interesting question,
4　Detective. I'm certain it must be harder to tutor two
5　tooters to toot than it is to toot the flute.
6　PENNY PIPER: I agree. Now back to the bitter batter. Was
7　there anyone here besides you and the baker, Betty
8　Botter?
9　TERRY TOOTER: *(Considers this.)* Well, come to think of
10　it, there was the stocky stockboy.
11　PENNY PIPER: The stocky stockboy?
12　TERRY TOOTER: Yes, Fuzzy-Wuzzy, the rather stocky
13　stockboy. He was here. He happens to be a bear, by
14　the way.
15　PENNY PIPER: Fuzzy-Wuzzy is a bear?
16　TERRY TOOTER: Yes. But, oddly enough, Fuzzy-Wuzzy
17　has no hair, which is extremely rare for a bear, I
18　declare.
19　PENNY PIPER: A bear with no hair? That is rare. Very
20　curious. He wasn't very fuzzy, was he?
21　TERRY TOOTER: Not at all.
22　PENNY PIPER: Hmmmm. *(Begins pacing.)* Did it ever
23　occur to you that Fuzzy-Wuzzy might not be a bear at
24　all?
25　TERRY TOOTER: Not a bear? Well, I didn't want to stare.
26　So, what are you getting at?
27　PENNY PIPER: Maybe he told you he was a bear to hide
28　his true identity. Look at it this way. If two witches
29　were watching two watches, which witch would
30　watch which watch?
31　TERRY TOOTER: *(Thinks a minute.)* I have no idea.
32　PENNY PIPER: Never mind! It's not important. We have
33　got to find this backstabbing bear! If my instincts
34　serve me right, I'll bet that stocky stockboy has a
35　whole storeroom filled with bitter butter, and he's

1   out to spoil the bakery's better batter.
2   **TERRY TOOTER: Brilliant, Detective!** *(PENNY PIPER*
3   *begins to cough.)* **Oh, dear. Is it your allergies?**
4   **PENNY PIPER: Yes, but I'll be fine. Just a little tickle in my**
5   **throat from all the flour. Don't worry, it's not the**
6   **cough that carries you off, but the coffin they carry**
7   **you off in! Now, let's go find that bear!** *(They exit in a*
8   *flurry. Curtain.)*
9
10
11 **Reference – Tongue Twisters:**
12 Various traditional tongue-twisters.

9. The Jig Is Up!

Cast of Characters:

Little JOHNNY Green, the neighborhood bad boy.

OFFICER JONES, the local authority.

Little TOMMY Stout, a boy scout.

Props:

Table and chairs set at Center Stage.

Scene:

An interrogation room at the local police station.

1   *(JOHNNY is sitting on one side of a bare table. He talks*
2   *like a tough guy, with questionable grammar. OFFICER*
3   *JONES paces the room as the interrogation takes place.*
4   *This interrogation has apparently been going on for a*
5   *while.)*
6   **OFFICER JONES:** *(Leaning in on the table with both hands.*
7   *Speaks firmly to JOHNNY.)* **Look, Johnny, the jig is up!**
8   **Your reign of terror is over! You hear me, *over!* Now,**
9   **confess to this heinous crime so we can all get on with**
10   **our lives.**
11   **JOHNNY:** *(Snickers.)* **You must be kidding. You got nothin' on**
12   **me, Officer. I'm clean.**
13   **OFFICER JONES: Clean? I don't think so, Johnny. Not this**
14   **time. We know what you did!**
15   **JOHNNY:** *(With mock innocence)* **What? What'd I do? I been**
16   **home with my mommy all day long.**
17   **OFFICER JONES: That's a lie, Johnny, and you know it!**
18   **You've been causing trouble in this town for years, and**
19   **we finally gotcha! Putting innocent little pussycats into**
20   **wells. That's pretty low, Johnny. Pretty low! What were**
21   **you thinking?**
22   **JOHNNY: I didn't do it! Besides, it was just an old pussycat.**

1   Who cares!

2   OFFICER JONES: Who cares? Well, for your information, I

3   care! And your father cares! That pussycat was your

4   father's prize mouser! He could catch ten or twelve

5   mice a day! You don't find a barn cat like that just

6   anywhere. Your father loved that cat!

7   JOHNNY: *(Not impressed)* Yeah, yeah. I heard all about that

8   stupid cat every day of my life! *(Imitating his father,*

9   *sarcastically)* "That's some great cat! If only you could

10   work as hard as that cat does, Johnny. Then you'd

11   really be worth something, you good-for-nothing

12   kid." So what? It's just a stupid cat.

13   OFFICER JONES: Oh, so that's it, huh, Johnny? You were

14   jealous of your father's cat? You thought your father

15   liked the cat better than he liked his own son? Is that

16   it, Johnny?

17   JOHNNY: I didn't say nothin' like that!

18   OFFICER JONES: Come on, Johnny, admit it. You threw

19   the pussycat down the well because you were jealous

20   of the cat and mad at your father. Is that it?

21   JOHNNY: I didn't do no such thing. I never cared about

22   that stupid cat. I just ignored him. You can't prove

23   that I tried to hurt him!

24   OFFICER JONES: Well, guess what, Johnny? It doesn't

25   matter if you confess to this crime.

26   JOHNNY: *(Confused)* It don't?

27   OFFICER JONES: No, it doesn't matter 'cause we've got a

28   witness.

29   JOHNNY: *(Surprised)* A witness?

30   OFFICER JONES: Yes, Johnny, a witness. Someone saw you

31   put that pussycat in the well. Someone who knows

32   you very well.

33   JOHNNY: What are you talkin' 'bout? Nobody saw me do

34   nothin'!

35   OFFICER JONES: *(Calling Off-stage.)* Bring in the witness!

1   (*TOMMY enters the interrogation room. JOHNNY*
2   *jumps out of his chair and points at TOMMY.*)
3   **JOHNNY: You! What are you doin' here?**
4   **OFFICER JONES:** (*To JOHNNY*) **Sit down and behave**
5   **yourself, Mr. Green.** (*JOHNNY sits, against his will.*)
6   **Have a seat, Mr. Stout.** (*TOMMY takes a seat at the table*
7   *across from JOHNNY. OFFICER JONES remains*
8   *standing. The two BOYS glare at each other.*) **I assume**
9   **you two gentlemen know each other?**
10   **TOMMY: Yeah. I know him.**
11   **JOHNNY: Yeah, I know this bum.** (*Both BOYS jump to their*
12   *feet as if ready to fight.*)
13   **OFFICER JONES: Hey, hey. Take it easy, both of you! Sit**
14   **down. You — Johnny — watch your language!** (*Both*
15   *BOYS sit down slowly, staring at each other.*) **There**
16   **seems to be some bad blood between you boys.**
17   **JOHNNY: You could say that. Mr. Goody Two-Shoes over**
18   **there never does nothin' wrong. Everybody loves**
19   **him. Eagle Scout, president of the class, and total**
20   **nerd!**
21   **TOMMY: Why, you! It's not my fault you want to be a**
22   **juvenile delinquent! You were always making bad**
23   **choices, ever since we were kids. You get yourself**
24   **into trouble. Don't blame me!** (*TOMMY and JOHNNY*
25   *start to argue with each other at the same time.*
26   *OFFICER JONES stops them.*)
27   **OFFICER JONES: All right! That's enough! Stop it, both of**
28   **you! Break it up!** (*The BOYS gradually stop arguing.*)
29   **OFFICER JONES: That's better! Now, Tommy, tell me, in**
30   **your own words, what you saw at the old well.**
31   **TOMMY: Well, I was walking through the woods when I**
32   **noticed someone lurking around over by the well.**
33   **Someone was crouching behind the trees and**
34   **darting from one tree to another.**
35   **OFFICER JONES: Go on.**

1 TOMMY: I ducked behind a tree myself so I could watch
2   what was going on. Then I saw a boy come out from
3   behind the well with a sack in his hands. He looked
4   around, to make sure he was alone, I suppose. I
5   watched him. It was Little Johnny Green, all right. I
6   saw him as plain as day!
7 OFFICER JONES: Go on.
8 TOMMY: He put down the sack and reached inside. Then I
9   saw him pull out his father's cat. He laughed out loud
10   as he dropped the cat into the well. It was terrible!
11 JOHNNY: *(To TOMMY)* Why, you! *(To OFFICER JONES)* He's
12   lying, Officer! I didn't see nobody up at that well!
13 OFFICER JONES: *(Turning to JOHNNY)* What did you say?
14 JOHNNY: *(Not realizing that he has given himself away.)* I'm
15   telling you! There was nobody else up at that well.
16   *(Stops.)* Oops.
17 OFFICER JONES: Oops is right, Johnny. That's a
18   confession if I've ever heard one!
19 TOMMY: And just so you know, Johnny, I fished that cat
20   out of the well as soon as you ran down the hill. He
21   was soaking wet but no worse for wear! I took him
22   back to your father's farm where he can chase mice
23   for many good years to come.
24 JOHNNY: *(Jumping to his feet)* Why, you! Why don't you
25   mind your own business for once! Nobody asked you
26   to help that cat!
27 OFFICER JONES: All right, Johnny. That's enough! *(Takes*
28   *JOHNNY's arm and starts to usher him out.)* I've got a
29   little community service in mind for you at the
30   Humane Society. You can help take care of all the
31   poor cats at the shelter. Maybe that will teach you to
32   respect animals.
33 TOMMY: *(Calling after JOHNNY)* Good-bye, Johnny! See you
34   later — after you clean out those litter boxes! *(Curtain.)*

1   **Reference — Nursery Rhyme:**
2   "Ding, dong, bell,
3   Pussy's in the well.
4   Who put her in?
5   Little Johnny Green.
6   Who pulled her out?
7   Little Tommy Stout.
8   What a naughty boy was that,
9   To try to drown poor pussycat,
10   Who ne'er did him any harm,
11   But killed all the mice in the farmer's barn."

10. A Perennial Problem

Cast of Characters:

MARY-MARY, who is quite contrary most of the time.

PETER-PETER, the selfish, hoarding pumpkin-eater.

Props:

Plants, a watering can, and a table set at Center Stage to hold the plants.

Scene:

Peter-Peter's plant nursery.

1   *(As the scene begins, PETER-PETER is watering and*
2   *tending several potted plants. He is very devoted to his*
3   *beautiful plants. MARY-MARY enters. She is shopping for*
4   *some new plants for her unusual garden.)*
5   **PETER-PETER:** *(To MARY-MARY)* **Hello. Can I help you find**
6   **anything?**
7   **MARY-MARY: No, thank you. I'm just looking.**
8   **PETER-PETER: All right. Just let me know if I can help.**
9   **MARY-MARY: I never need help.**
10   **PETER-PETER: Oh. All right.** *(There is a pause as PETER-*
11   *PETER continues watering and MARY-MARY continues*
12   *looking around. Finally, PETER-PETER breaks the*
13   *silence.)* **Lovely weather we're having, isn't it?**
14   **MARY-MARY: You think this is lovely weather? I think it's**
15   **terrible, all gloomy and rainy.**
16   **PETER-PETER: Oh. Well, it's good weather for ducks**
17   **anyway.** *(Laughs.)*
18   **MARY-MARY:** *(Glares at PETER-PETER.)* **Very funny. I don't**
19   **care for ducks.**
20   **PETER-PETER:** *(Realizes that MARY-MARY is particularly*
21   *grumpy.)* **How can anyone not like ducks? They are**
22   **beautiful and useful creatures who eat the slugs out of**

1   our gardens.

2 **MARY-MARY: I think they squawk too much!** *(PETER-*

3   *PETER thinks he has realized something about MARY-*

4   *MARY. So he tries an experiment with her. He calls out*

5   *some words to test her.)*

6 **PETER-PETER:** *(To MARY-MARY)* **Up!**

7 **MARY-MARY:** *(Can't help but respond with the opposite.)*

8   **Down!**

9 **PETER-PETER: Right!**

10 **MARY-MARY: Wrong!**

11 **PETER-PETER: Black!**

12 **MARY-MARY: White!**

13 **PETER-PETER: Here!**

14 **MARY-MARY: There!**

15 **PETER-PETER: So it is you! The famous Mary-Mary! I've**

16   **heard about you.**

17 **MARY-MARY: No, you haven't.**

18 **PETER-PETER: Yes, I have.**

19 **MARY-MARY: No, you haven't.**

20 **PETER-PETER: I most certainly have.** *(Stops her as she*

21   *opens her mouth.)* **Stop!**

22 **MARY-MARY: Stop what?**

23 **PETER-PETER: You were going to disagree with me again.**

24 **MARY-MARY: No, I wasn't.**

25 **PETER-PETER: Yes, you were.**

26 **MARY-MARY: No, I —**

27 **PETER-PETER:** *(Stopping her again)* **Stop! That's amazing.**

28   **You truly are the most contrary person I've ever met.**

29 **MARY-MARY: No, I'm not.**

30 **PETER-PETER: Yes, you are! That's where you got your**

31   **nickname, "Mary, Mary, quite contrary." Because you**

32   **disagree with everything anybody has to say! That's**

33   **quite a strange problem.**

34 **MARY-MARY: No, it's not.**

35 **PETER-PETER: Well, I think it is.**

1 MARY-MARY: No, it's —

2 PETER-PETER: *(Stopping her again)* **Stop! It's all right. You**
3 **don't have to be contrary with me.**

4 MARY-MARY: **Yes, I do.**

5 PETER-PETER: **No, you don't.** *(Puts his hands up to stop*
6 *her.)* **Now, let's just try to have a normal conversation.**
7 **Would that be all right?**

8 MARY-MARY: *(Struggles not to be contrary and speaks very*
9 *slowly.)* **All right.**

10 PETER-PETER: **Very good! You see? You can agree with**
11 **someone else from time to time.**

12 MARY-MARY: *(Answering quickly)* **No, I can't.**

13 PETER-PETER: **Sure you can! Now, let's just take it slow.**
14 **How can I help you?**

15 MARY-MARY: *(Trying very hard not to be contrary)* **I would**
16 **like some plants for my garden, please.**

17 PETER-PETER: **Now we're getting somewhere! Plants for**
18 **your garden. May I call you Mary? Or do you prefer**
19 **Mary-Mary?**

20 MARY-MARY: **I actually prefer Mary-Mary. It makes me**
21 **sound twice as important. I hope you don't mind.**

22 PETER-PETER: **Of course not. I completely understand. I**
23 **myself go by my full name — Peter-Peter. Adds a bit of**
24 **class, don't you think?**

25 MARY-MARY: **I do.**

26 PETER-PETER: **Now, you see there? We are agreeing on**
27 **something.**

28 MARY-MARY: **I guess we are.** *(Smiles.)*

29 PETER-PETER: **Now, what kind of flowers do you have**
30 **growing in your garden currently?**

31 MARY-MARY: **Well, let's see. I have silver bells.**

32 PETER-PETER: **Oh, that's lovely.**

33 MARY-MARY: **And cockle shells.**

34 PETER-PETER: **Cockle shells? Those aren't really flowers,**
35 **are they?**

1 MARY-MARY: Yes, they are.
2 PETER-PETER: No, they're not. Cockleshells are mollusks
3 — like clams and oysters. They grow in the sea.
4 MARY-MARY: Well, they're growing in my garden, too!
5 PETER-PETER: All right, all right. Let's not argue about it.
6 We were doing so well. What other plants do you
7 have?
8 MARY-MARY: I have pretty maids.
9 PETER-PETER: Pretty maids? Is that a kind of perennial?
10 I've never heard of that plant before.
11 MARY-MARY: I'm not sure if they are perennials, but
12 they're lovely and they stand all in a row.
13 PETER-PETER: Hmmmm, I thought I knew every plant
14 there was. What do they look like?
15 MARY-MARY: Well, they are about this tall. *(Holds her*
16 *hand up to her own height.)* And they wear lovely
17 dresses and petticoats.
18 PETER-PETER: Dresses and petticoats? Like real girls? Do
19 you mean you have real girls standing in your
20 garden?
21 MARY-MARY: *(Doesn't seem to see anything wrong with*
22 *this.)* Yes. Why? They are very pretty. They stand right
23 behind the marigolds in a nice straight line.
24 PETER-PETER: How do you get them to stay there?
25 MARY-MARY: I simply ask them nicely. Why? Is that a
26 problem?
27 PETER-PETER: Well, it doesn't seem quite right somehow.
28 I've never heard of a garden like yours before. It is
29 certainly unconventional.
30 MARY-MARY: Well, you know I like to be different.
31 PETER-PETER: I can see that. So, what kind of "plants"
32 are you looking for today?
33 MARY-MARY: *(Looks around the shop.)* I was thinking
34 about growing a few vegetables. Perhaps pumpkins.
35 PETER-PETER: Pumpkins?

1　MARY-MARY: Yes, I thought I could grow some nice big
2　　　pumpkins. Then I can have pumpkin soup, pumpkin
3　　　bread, and pumpkin pie. Do you have any pumpkin
4　　　plants for sale?
5　PETER-PETER: *(Getting noticeably nervous)* Uh, no. No
6　　　pumpkins. What about zucchini or spaghetti squash,
7　　　something delicious like that?
8　MARY-MARY: Well, those are certainly good choices, too,
9　　　but I think I'd rather grow some nice round
10　　　pumpkins.
11　PETER-PETER: Well, I'm sorry, but we don't have any
12　　　pumpkin plants, but thank you for coming in. *(Starts*
13　　　*to push MARY-MARY toward the exit. She stops him.)*
14　MARY-MARY: What do you mean you don't have any
15　　　pumpkin plants? This is a plant nursery. You must
16　　　have at least one pumpkin plant around here.
17　PETER-PETER: *(A curious change has come over him.)* No,
18　　　no, I'm sorry. I can't share any of the pumpkin plants.
19　　　They're mine. All mine!
20　MARY-MARY: Why do you need so many pumpkin plants?
21　　　Couldn't I buy just one little seed? I'll start it myself.
22　PETER-PETER: No! No, I can't sell even one little seed. I
23　　　might starve to death. They are all I eat — pumpkins!
24　　　Morning, noon and night — pumpkins! All right, I
25　　　admit it. I'm a pumpkin-eater! I eat pumpkins. I built
26　　　my house with a pumpkin. I drive a pumpkin. I can't
27　　　live without pumpkins, and I refuse to share my
28　　　pumpkins with anyone! Even the famous Mary-Mary.
29　MARY-MARY: I thought your name sounded familiar! So,
30　　　you are the very selfish Peter-Peter, the pumpkin-
31　　　eater. I've heard about you — living in pumpkins,
32　　　eating pumpkins, hoarding pumpkins. You are
33　　　totally obsessed with pumpkins!
34　PETER-PETER: Pumpkins are my friends! No one else can
35　　　have them.

1 MARY-MARY: Oh, really? And you think I have a problem
2 because I disagree with people? Look in the mirror,
3 buddy! You could use a few sessions on the
4 therapist's couch yourself, if you know what I mean.
5 Thanks for your help, but I'll purchase my pumpkin
6 seeds elsewhere and I'll grow the biggest, most
7 beautiful pumpkins you've ever seen. Ta-ta! *(Exits*
8 *with her nose in the air.)*
9 PETER-PETER: *(Calling after her)* That's just fine, Mary-
10 Mary! You try to grow big, healthy pumpkins in that
11 crazy garden of yours! They'll never sprout. Do you
12 hear me? They'll never grow for you! *(Curtain.)*
13
14
15 **Reference — Nursery Rhymes:**
16 "Peter, Peter, pumpkin-eater.
17 Had a wife and couldn't keep her.
18 Put her in a pumpkin shell
19 And there he kept her very well."
20
21 **And:**
22 "Mary, Mary, quite contrary,
23 How does your garden grow?
24 With silver bells and cockle shells,
25 And little maids all in a row."

Scenes for
Five to Twenty
Actors

11. Family Showdown

Cast of Characters:

ROGER DAWSON, the host of the TV game show *Family Showdown.*

PAPA BEAR, the head of the Three Bears family.

MAMA BEAR, the mother of the Three Bears family.

BABY BEAR, the youngest of the Three Bears family.

GOLDILOCKS, the fourth member of the Three Bears family with long and curly blonde hair.

GRUMPY, the head of the Dwarf family.

HAPPY, the second member of the Dwarf family.

SLEEPY, the third member of the Dwarf family.

SNOW WHITE, the fourth member of the Dwarf family.

BAND, five kazoo-playing musicians who double as card-holders for the game show.

Props:

Five handkerchiefs, five kazoos, and five large cards numbered 1-5 with answers written on the backs.

Scene:

The TV set for the game show, *Family Showdown.* Place two tables On-stage. One at Stage Right and one at Stage Left. Place a buzzer or push-button bell on each table. You will also need the sound effect of a ticking clock.

1	*(On one side of the stage stands the THREE BEARS*
2	*FAMILY. On the other side of the stage stands the DWARF*
3	*FAMILY. The scene opens with the BAND playing the*
4	Family Showdown *theme song on their kazoos. For the*
5	*theme song, choose a song all the BAND members know*
6	*and can play on kazoos. During the theme song, ROGER*
7	*DAWSON comes prancing onto the set and bows several*
8	*times to the audience.)*

1　ROGER DAWSON: *(To the audience)* **Welcome! Welcome,**
2　　　**everybody! I am your host ...**
3　ALL: *(Together)* **Roger Dawson!**
4　ROGER DAWSON: **That's right! And it's time to play ...**
5　ALL: *(Together again)* **The Family Showdown!** *(The THREE*
6　　　*BEARS FAMILY and the DWARF FAMILY clap and cheer.*
7　　　*As the music and cheering settle down, ROGER*
8　　　*DAWSON crosses to the THREE BEARS FAMILY.)*
9　ROGER DAWSON: **Let's get started by welcoming our first**
10　　　**family. Let me introduce to you − the Three Bears**
11　　　**Family! And you, sir, are Papa Bear. Correct?**
12　PAPA BEAR: *(Stuttering nervously into his microphone)* **Th-**
13　　　**th-that's correct, Roger.** *(Waves shyly to the audience.)*
14　ROGER DAWSON: **Well, Papa Bear, would you like to**
15　　　**introduce the rest of your family?**
16　PAPA BEAR: **Roger, this is Mama Bear, my better half.**
17　　　*(MAMA BEAR waves to the audience. ROGER DAWSON*
18　　　*takes her hand and kisses it graciously.)*
19　ROGER DAWSON: *(Gushing with charm)* **M'lady, it is a**
20　　　**pleasure to meet you.** *(MAMA BEAR giggles, blushing*
21　　　*at his attentions.)*
22　PAPA BEAR: **And this is Baby Bear, my youngest.**
23　ROGER DAWSON: **Hey, little dude, what's happening?**
24　　　*(ROGER DAWSON attempts a very complicated*
25　　　*handshake with BABY BEAR, who tries his or her best*
26　　　*to follow along, but can't quite figure it out.)*
27　PAPA BEAR: *(Unenthusiastically)* **And this is Goldilocks.**
28　　　*(GOLDILOCKS is thrilled to be on TV. She grabs ROGER*
29　　　*DAWSON's hand and shakes it vigorously. All the time,*
30　　　*she manages to keep smiling at the audience and*
31　　　*waving vigorously.)*
32　ROGER DAWSON: *(With great charm)* **Goldilocks,**
33　　　**delighted to meet you. I just love your hairdo.**
34　GOLDILOCKS: *(Very excited)* **Oh, thanks, Roger. My hair is**
35　　　**naturally blonde, curly, and beautiful. I'm so lucky.**

1   **Just wash, scrunch, and go!** *(Laughs and waves to the*
2   *audience again. PAPA BEAR, MAMA BEAR, and BABY*
3   *BEAR roll their eyes and shake their heads in*
4   *embarrassment.)* **I am so thrilled to be here! I love**
5   ***Family Showdown.* I watch it every day!**
6   **ROGER DAWSON: That's wonderful, Miss Locks. I must**
7   **say, you don't really resemble the rest of the Three**
8   **Bears family. Exactly how are you related to them?**
9   **GOLDILOCKS: Well, that's a funny story, Roger –**
10 **PAPA BEAR:** *(Quickly interrupting her)* **Goldilocks is a**
11   **distant relative. Very distant.**
12 **MAMA BEAR: She just recently found our home in the**
13   **woods.**
14 **BABY BEAR: Yeah. She just sort of dropped in one day and**
15   **made herself at home.**
16 **ROGER DAWSON: Well, that's just wonderful. Families**
17   **should be together, that's what I always say.** *(The*
18   *THREE BEARS force polite smiles toward ROGER*
19   *DAWSON, as he crosses the stage.)* **Now let's meet the**
20   **Dorf Family!**
21 **GRUMPY: That's *Dwarf,* you nitwit. D-W-A-R-F. Dwarf . We**
22   **are the Dwarf family – not the Dorf Family.**
23 **ROGER DAWSON: Oh, I am so sorry. That's the Dwarf**
24   **Family. And this is the head of the family, Grumpy**
25   **Dorf.** *(Says it wrong again.)*
26 **GRUMPY:** *(Getting upset)* **Dad gum it! We are not the Dorf**
27   **Family! We are the Dwarf family! Get it right, will ya?**
28 **ROGER DAWSON: Oh boy, somebody sure got up on the**
29   **wrong side of the bed this morning.** *(The BAND and*
30   *the THREE BEARS FAMILY laugh at ROGER DAWSON's*
31   *witty remarks.)* **I'll bet that's why they call you**
32   **Grumpy, isn't it?**
33 **GRUMPY:** *(Crosses his arms and gives ROGER DAWSON a*
34   *dirty look.)* **What's that supposed to mean? You a wise**
35   **guy or somethin'? My mother named me Grumpy**

1   after my great-grandfather Grumpfield Q. Dwarf, the
2   **first.** *(Shakes his fist at ROGER DAWSON, who pretends*
3   *to be afraid of him.)* **Why, you smart-alecky TV actor! I**
4   **oughta knock your block off.**
5 ROGER DAWSON: *(Laughs toward the audience.)* **What a**
6   **kidder! I love that in a contestant. So, Mister Dorf,**
7   **could you introduce us to the rest of your family?** *(At*
8   *hearing the name "Dorf" again, GRUMPY throws his*
9   *hands in the air, puts his hands on his hips and turns*
10   *his back on ROGER DAWSON. HAPPY jumps in quickly,*
11   *with a huge, toothy grin on his face.)*
12 HAPPY: **I'm Happy, Mr. Dawson!**
13 ROGER DAWSON: *(Shaking HAPPY's hand)* **Oh, well I am**
14   **happy, too!**
15 HAPPY: **No, I mean my name is Happy. Happy Dwarf. We**
16   **are so glad to be here on** *Family Showdown.* *(Motions*
17   *to SLEEPY.)* **This is our brother, Sleepy.** *(During the*
18   *previous conversation, SLEEPY has slowly lowered his*
19   *head onto the table in front of him. When he is*
20   *introduced, he begins to snore loudly, without lifting*
21   *his head.)*
22 ROGER DAWSON: **Somebody must be bored!** *(The BAND*
23   *laughs out loud again.)*
24 HAPPY: **Oh, no. He just falls asleep from time to time.**
25   *(Nudges SLEEPY to wake him up.)* **Sleepy.** *Sleepy!* **Wake**
26   **up. We're on television.**
27 SLEEPY: *(Suddenly opens his eyes and stands up straight.)*
28   **Huh? What? I'm awake! I'm awake!**
29 ROGER DAWSON: **Well, this should be a lively game.**
30   *(Moves down to SNOW WHITE.)* **And who are you, my**
31   **dear?**
32 SNOW WHITE: *(Sweetly)* **My name is Snow White.** *(She*
33   *holds out her hand to ROGER DAWSON.)* **It's just**
34   **wonderful to meet you, Mr. Dawson.**
35 ROGER DAWSON: **The pleasure is all mine.** *(Kisses her*

1   *hand then looks over at GOLDILOCKS.)* **You know,**
2   **Miss White, neither you nor Miss Locks has much of**
3   **a family resemblance to the other members of your**
4   **families.**
5 **SNOW WHITE: Well, Roger, that's a funny story ...**
6 **GRUMPY:** *(Turning around quickly to ROGER DAWSON)*
7   **Snow White is also a distant relative.**
8 **HAPPY: Yes. She sort of dropped in on us one day, too. Just**
9   **like Miss Locks did.**
10 **SLEEPY: That's right.** *(Yawns.)* **She just found our little**
11   **house in the woods and made herself at home.** *(Starts*
12   *to fall back to sleep, but HAPPY catches him.)*
13 **ROGER DAWSON: How wonderful. Family stories like**
14   **that just touch my heart.** *(Sniffs and dabs his eyes with*
15   *a handkerchief. The BAND members each pull out*
16   *handkerchiefs and dab their tears. ROGER DAWSON*
17   *recovers suddenly and announces in a big voice.)* **Let's**
18   **play *Family Showdown!*** *(The BAND starts playing the*
19   *lively theme song on their kazoos. Everybody claps and*
20   *cheers. PAPA BEAR and GRUMPY cross to either side of*
21   *the center podium with ROGER DAWSON Upstage*
22   *between them. PAPA BEAR and GRUMPY shake hands.*
23   *There is a button in front of PAPA BEAR and a button in*
24   *front of GRUMPY. They each hold one hand just above*
25   *their button, ready to slap it down. ROGER DAWSON*
26   *holds a large card in his hand with the question on it.*
27   *The music subsides as ROGER DAWSON begins.)* **Now,**
28   **you all know how we play the game. We polled our**
29   **studio audience to find the most popular answers to**
30   **the following question. The top five answers are on**
31   **the board.** *(The BAND stands. Each member is holding*
32   *a sheet of paper with one of the top five answers on it.*
33   *The sides facing the audience at this point read, "1,"*
34   *"2," "3," "4," and "5." The papers will be flipped to show*
35   *the answers one at a time when ROGER DAWSON calls*

1   *for them.)* **Papa Bear and Grumpy Dorf, you are up!**
2   *(GRUMPY throws his hands in the air again. He is ready*
3   *to quit but the other members of his team encourage*
4   *him to go on. He turns back to listen to ROGER*
5   *DAWSON.)* **If you think you know the number-one**
6   **answer to the question, slap your button, and the first**
7   **one to ring his buzzer will give me the answer. If you**
8   **do not guess the number-one answer, your opponent**
9   **will have a chance to steal. Do you understand the**
10   **rules?**
11 **PAPA BEAR:** *(Answering at the same time as GRUMPY)* **We**
12   **understand.**
13 **GRUMPY:** *(Answering at the same time as PAPA BEAR)* **Yeah,**
14   **we got it.**
15 **ROGER DAWSON: All right, here is the question.** *(Speaks*
16   *slowly and carefully.)* **What is your biggest pet peeve?**
17   *(Both GRUMPY and PAPA BEAR slam their hands on*
18   *their buttons.)* **Papa Bear, you were first. What did our**
19   **studio audience say was their top answer to the**
20   **question, "What is your biggest pet peeve?"**
21 **PAPA BEAR: Roger, I believe the number one pet peeve**
22   **would be, "Having a little girl break into your house**
23   **and sit on your chairs."** *(MAMA BEAR and BABY BEAR*
24   *cheer and clap. GOLDILOCKS looks confused.)*
25 **MAMA BEAR:** *(Simultaneously with BABY BEAR)* **Good**
26   **answer, Papa Bear.**
27 **BABY BEAR:** *(Simultaneously with MAMA BEAR)* **Way to go,**
28   **Papa Bear!**
29 **ROGER DAWSON: All right. You said, "Having a little girl**
30   **break into your house and sit on your chairs." Is**
31   **"Having a little girl break into your house and sit on**
32   **your chairs" on the list?** *(The BAND member who*
33   *holds the "5" card turns around his card, which reads,*
34   *"Having a little girl break into your house and sit on*
35   *your chairs.")* **Papa Bear, you have chosen the fifth**

1 most popular answer to the question. There are four
2 answers that have received more votes than your
3 answer. Grumpy, if you can give us one of the first
4 four answers, then your family will have a chance to
5 steal. What is your answer?
6 GRUMPY: Roger, I think the number-one answer is,
7 "Having a girl break into your house and clean it
8 from top to bottom!"
9 ROGER DAWSON: Really? That's your biggest pet peeve?
10 GRUMPY: Ooh, it drives me crazy!
11 ROGER DAWSON: *(Shrugs.)* All right. Show us, "Having a
12 girl break into your house and clean it from top to
13 bottom!" *(The BAND member holding the "4" card*
14 *turns it over to reveal GRUMPY's answer: "Having a girl*
15 *break into your house and clean it from top to bottom.")*
16 I can't believe it. Evidently there are a lot of people in
17 the studio audience who have had the same problem.
18 But there are three answers that got even more votes.
19 The Dorf family can decide whether to pass or play.
20 What will it be? Will you try to guess the rest of the
21 answers, or pass to the Three Bears family? *(The*
22 *DWARF FAMILY huddles together behind their table,*
23 *discussing the situation. They break, and GRUMPY*
24 *addresses ROGER DAWSON.)*
25 GRUMPY: The Dwarf family has decided to pass, Roger.
26 ROGER DAWSON: All righty then. The Dorf family has
27 passed to the Three Bears family. Mama Bear, it's
28 your turn. What do you think is the top answer to the
29 question, "What is your biggest pet peeve?"
30 MAMA BEAR: I think it's quite obvious what the number-
31 one answer would have to be. *(Starts to get emotional.)*
32 "Little girls who break into your house when you
33 have gone out for a nice little walk and eat all your
34 porridge while it is supposed to be cooling."
35 PAPA BEAR and BABY BEAR: *(Cheer her on.)* Good answer,

1   **Mama Bear! Good answer.** *(GOLDILOCKS looks*
2   *confused again.)*
3   **ROGER DAWSON:** *(In disbelief)* **Really? That's your**
4   **number-one answer? And you think it's also the**
5   **number one answer of all the members of our studio**
6   **audience out there.**
7   **MAMA BEAR: I can't think of anything more annoying**
8   **than that.**
9   **ROGER DAWSON:** *(Shrugs.)* **OK, it's up to you. Show me the**
10   **answer, "Little girls who break into your house when**
11   **you have gone out for a nice little walk and eat all**
12   **your porridge while it is supposed to be cooling."** *(The*
13   *BAND member with the "3" card turns over his/her*
14   *card which reads, "Little girls who break into your*
15   *house when you have gone out for a nice little walk and*
16   *eat all your porridge while it is supposed to be cooling."*
17   *Cheering erupts in the THREE BEARS FAMILY. The*
18   *BAND plays the lively theme song on their kazoos. The*
19   *DWARF FAMILY looks a little worried as they huddle*
20   *together, trying to come up with the number-one*
21   *answer. ROGER DAWSON moves down the line to BABY*
22   *BEAR.)* **Baby Bear, we have come to you. There are two**
23   **more answers on the board. What do you think is the**
24   **studio audience's number-one answer to this**
25   **question?** *(Reads the question again.)* **"What is your**
26   **biggest pet peeve?"**
27 **BABY BEAR:** *(Looks nervous.)* **Well, Roger, I think the**
28   **studio audience would have to say, "Little girls who**
29   **break into your house when you have gone out for a**
30   **nice little walk to let your porridge cool and take a**
31   **nap in your bed, mess up all the covers, and throw**
32   **your pillows on the floor."**
33 **PAPA BEAR and MAMA BEAR:** *(Ad-lib)* **Good answer, Baby**
34   **Bear! Good answer!** *(GOLDILOCKS is getting more and*
35   *more upset.)*

1   **ROGER DAWSON:** *(In disbelief)* **Really? That's your final**
2   **answer?**
3   **BABY BEAR:** *(Smiles confidently.)* **That's my final answer,**
4   **Roger.**
5   **ROGER DAWSON: OK. Show us, "Little girls who break**
6   **into your house when you have gone out for a nice**
7   **little walk to let your porridge cool and take a nap in**
8   **your bed, mess up all the covers, and throw your**
9   **pillows on the floor."** *(The BAND member with the "2"*
10   *card turns his/hers over to reveal the answer, "Little*
11   *girls who break into your house when you have gone*
12   *out for a nice little walk to let your porridge cool and*
13   *take a nap in your bed, mess up all the covers, and*
14   *throw your pillows on the floor." Celebration erupts*
15   *from the THREE BEARS. GOLDILOCKS stands with*
16   *her arms crossed, frowning. ROGER DAWSON moves*
17   *on down the row to GOLDILOCKS.)*
18   **ROGER DAWSON: Miss Locks, you don't look very happy.**
19   **What's wrong? Your team is winning.**
20   **GOLDILOCKS: I know our team is winning, but I don't**
21   **particularly like the answers.**
22   **ROGER DAWSON: Well, now it's your turn. Do you think**
23   **you have the number-one answer?**
24   **GOLDILOCKS: Yes, Roger, I do believe I know the number-**
25   **one answer to the question.**
26   **ROGER DAWSON: And what is your answer?**
27   **GOLDILOCKS: "Bears who try to frighten little girls and**
28   **chase them out of their houses."** *(Smiles broadly.)*
29   **ROGER DAWSON: "Bears who try to frighten little girls**
30   **and chase them out of their houses?" That's your**
31   **answer? Really?**
32   **GOLDILOCKS:** *(Certain that she is right)* **Yes, that's my**
33   **answer.**
34   **ROGER DAWSON: Your final answer? "Bears who try to**
35   **frighten little girls and chase them out of their**

1 houses?" You're going to stick with that?
2 GOLDILOCKS: That is correct, Roger. *(PAPA BEAR, MAMA*
3 *BEAR, and BABY BEAR scowl at GOLDILOCKS*
4 *throughout this discussion.)*
5 ROGER DAWSON: You are certain that the majority of the
6 people in the studio audience said that "bears who
7 frighten little girls and chase them out of their
8 houses" is their *biggest* pet peeve? *(Dramatically)*
9 Their *biggest* pet peeve in the world!
10 GOLDILOCKS: I am sure of it. What else could it be?
11 ROGER DAWSON: *(Gives up.)* OK. Show me, "Bears who
12 try to frighten little girls and chase them out of their
13 houses." *(A buzzer sounds to indicate that this was not*
14 *the number-one answer. The THREE BEARS are*
15 *devastated and angry at GOLDILOCKS. On the other*
16 *hand, the DWARF FAMILY is ecstatic.)* The Dorf family
17 has a chance to win the game. *(HAPPY, SLEEPY, and*
18 *SNOW WHITE have to hold back the angry GRUMPY*
19 *when ROGER DAWSON calls them the "Dorf" family*
20 *again.)* Happy, it's your turn. What do you think the
21 number-one answer is?
22 HAPPY: Roger, I think the number-one pet peeve is,
23 "Cranky witches."
24 ROGER DAWSON: Of course it is. Happy says, "Cranky
25 witches." Is "cranky witches" the number-one
26 answer? *(The "wrong answer" buzzer sounds again.*
27 *ROGER DAWSON quickly turns to SLEEPY.)* Sleepy,
28 give us your number-one answer for "biggest pet
29 peeve."
30 SLEEPY: Roger, I would say the number-one pet peeve is,
31 "People throwing loud parties with singing, dancing,
32 and wild animals romping around the house while
33 you're trying to take a nap!"
34 ROGER DAWSON: Show me, "People throwing loud
35 parties with singing, dancing, and wild animals

1   **romping around the house while you're trying to**
2   **take a nap!"** *(The "wrong answer" buzzer sounds*
3   *again.)* **What a shock! It's not the top answer.** *(The*
4   *DWARF FAMILY is concerned but the THREE BEARS*
5   *FAMILY is getting excited.)* **All right, Snow, it's up to**
6   **you. Your team has one last chance to guess the**
7   **number-one answer, or the Bear family wins the**
8   **game. What is your answer to the question, "What is**
9   **your biggest pet peeve?"** *(A clock starts ticking. All the*
10   *contestants are nervously awaiting her answer.)*
11 **SNOW WHITE: Roger, I think I know what the studio**
12   **audience has chosen as their number-one answer.**
13 **ROGER DAWSON: Then please, I beg of you, tell us.**
14 **SNOW WHITE: The number-one answer is, "Poison apples**
15   **that make you fall asleep for a long time while**
16   **everyone thinks you're dead, so they lock you in a**
17   **crystal coffin and you have to lie there until some**
18   **guy who thinks he's Prince Charming happens**
19   **along, kisses you, wakes you up, and expects you to**
20   **just go off and get married without even knowing**
21   **him." That is the number-one pet peeve.**
22 **ROGER DAWSON:** *(Doesn't even question the answers*
23   *anymore. He turns slowly to the BAND.)* **Show me,**
24   **"Poison apples that make you fall asleep for a long**
25   **time while everyone thinks you're dead, so they lock**
26   **you in a crystal coffin and you have to lie there until**
27   **some guy who thinks he's Prince Charming happens**
28   **along, kisses you, wakes you up, and expects you to**
29   **just go off and get married without even knowing**
30   **him."** *(The BAND member holding the "1" card turns it*
31   *around to reveal the number-one answer which reads,*
32   *"Poison apples that make you fall asleep for a long time*
33   *while everyone thinks you're dead, so they lock you in*
34   *a crystal coffin and you have to lie there until some guy*
35   *who thinks he's Prince Charming happens along,*

1   kisses you, wakes you up, and expects you to just go off
2   and get married without even knowing him.")
3   **Unbelievable! The Dorf Family wins!** *(Celebration*
4   *erupts. The BAND joyously plays the* Family Showdown
5   *theme song on their kazoos. ROGER DAWSON throws*
6   *his cards up in the air in disbelief. The THREE BEARS*
7   *FAMILY argues among itself. GRUMPY, angry at being*
8   *called the "Dorf" family once again, chases ROGER*
9   *DAWSON around the tables. SLEEPY falls asleep on the*
10   *table. SNOW WHITE and HAPPY dance a little jig*
11   *together as the mayhem continues around them.*
12   *Curtain.)*
13
14
15   **Reference – Fairy Tales:**
16   The Story of "Goldilocks and the Three Bears"
17   The Story of "Snow White and the Seven Dwarfs"

12. The New Recruits

Cast of Characters:

SERGEANT, the head ant in charge of training the new recruits.

LITTLE ONE, a new, easily distracted ant recruit.

ANT RECRUITS, a troop of new ant recruits, still learning the basics of marching.

Props:

Whistle.

Scene:

The training ground for the ant recruits.

1   *(The new RECRUITS are learning how to function like an*
2   *efficient, ant-marching machine. From Off-stage we hear*
3   *the drill of the ANT RECRUITS moving closer.)*
4   **ANT RECRUITS:** *(Off-stage)* **Hup-two-three-four. Hup-two-**
5   **three-four!** *(They march onto the stage in single file,*
6   *following the SERGEANT.)* **Hup-two-three-four. Hup-**
7   **two-three-four. Left-Right. Left-Right.**
8   **SERGEANT:** *(Shouts out in rhythm.)* **There's none of the**
9   **enemy left, right?**
10 **ANT RECRUITS: Right-left. Right-left. The Sergeant is**
11 **always right-left. Right-left.** *(Start to become confused.*
12 *They are on the wrong foot.)* **No, left-right. Left-right.**
13 *(Become confused and start bumping into each other,*
14 *trying to go in different directions. SERGEANT blows a*
15 *whistle that he or she carries around the neck.)*
16 **SERGEANT: Halt! Halt!** *Stop!*
17 **ANT RECRUITS:** *(Shouting out randomly)* **Halt! Halt! Stop!**
18 *(Finally settle down and come to a standstill.)*
19 **SERGEANT: Line up!** *(ANT RECRUITS scramble back into one*
20 *straight line and stand at attention. SERGEANT paces*

1   *back and forth in front of the line as he or she addresses*
2   *the troops.)* **All right, recruits, straighten up! Come to**
3   **attention! That was the worst marching I have ever**
4   **seen. You were supposed to be marching one by one.**
5   **That's single file. I know you're just learning, but I**
6   **think you can do better than that! Can't you?**
7 **ANT RECRUITS:** *(Call out together.)* **Yes, sir.**
8 **SERGEANT: That's what I like to hear! Now, let's try that**
9   **maneuver again, shall we?**
10 **ANT RECRUITS: Yes, sir.**
11 **SERGEANT: I can't hear you!**
12 **ANT RECRUITS:** *(Louder)* **Yes, sir!**
13 **SERGEANT: That's more like it. Now, let's try again. One**
14   **by one, single file. Hup-two-three-four.** *(ANT*
15   *RECRUITS begin marching single file around the stage.)*
16 **ANT RECRUITS: Hup-two-three-four. Hup-two-three-four.**
17   **Hup-two-three-four. Hup-two-three-four.** *(As they*
18   *continue marching, LITTLE ONE, the last ant in line,*
19   *stops, sits down, and starts to suck his or her thumb as*
20   *the rest of the ANT RECRUITS continue to march.*
21   *SERGEANT sees LITTLE ONE and calls to the troops.)*
22 **SERGEANT: Halt!**
23 **ANT RECRUITS: Halt!**
24 **SERGEANT: Stop!** *(ANT RECRUITS come to a sloppy stop,*
25   *once again bumping into each other. They land in a*
26   *heap. SERGEANT slowly walks over to LITTLE ONE,*
27   *trying to remain calm.)* **What do you think you're**
28   **doing?**
29 **LITTLE ONE:** *(Looking up at the SERGEANT)* **Who, me?**
30 **SERGEANT: Yes, you. What do you think you're doing?**
31 **LITTLE ONE:** *(Looks around. It seems quite obvious.)* **I was**
32   **just taking a little rest and sucking my thumb. Is that**
33   **a problem?**
34 **SERGEANT: Is that a problem?** *Is that a problem?* **Yes,**
35   **that's a problem! You are supposed to be marching**

1   one by one with everyone else, but instead you're
2   sitting here sucking your thumb! What is your name,
3   recruit?
4 LITTLE ONE: My name is Little One.
5 SERGEANT: And what is your last name?
6 LITTLE ONE: Everyone just calls me Little One. You know,
7   Sarge, maybe we all should take a little break. I'm
8   sure the other ant recruits are tired, too. *(SERGEANT*
9   *looks sternly back at the pile of ANT RECRUITS.)*
10 SERGEANT: *(Speaks slowly.)* **Do you need a break, too?**
11   *(The ANT RECRUITS don't dare answer "yes." They*
12   *shake their heads vigorously "no.")*
13 LITTLE ONE: *(Stands up and walks over to the ANT*
14   *RECRUITS.)* **Oh, come on guys. We all could use a**
15   **little rest, right? Maybe take a quick siesta or snack**
16   **on some trail mix? We've been marching since**
17   **sunup.** *(Once again, the ANT RECRUITS shake their*
18   *heads vigorously "no.")*
19 SERGEANT: **Satisfied?** *Now, back in line!* *(The ANT*
20   *RECRUITS, including LITTLE ONE, get back into a*
21   *straight line, facing front.)* **This time we will practice**
22   **marching two by two. Line up! Two by two! Let's go,**
23   **let's go!** *(The ANT RECRUITS scramble into a two-by-*
24   *two formation and start to march again.)* **Hup-two-**
25   **three-four. Hup-two-three-four.**
26 ANT RECRUITS: **Hup-two-three-four. Hup-two-three-four.**
27   **Hup-two-three-four. Hup-two-three-four.** *(The ANT*
28   *RECRUITS march two by two around the stage. After*
29   *taking a tour around the stage, LITTLE ONE kneels*
30   *down on the floor and begins to work on tying his or*
31   *her shoelaces.)*
32 SERGEANT: **Halt! Stop!** *(The ANT RECRUITS stumble into*
33   *each other again as they come to a stop.)*
34 ANT RECRUITS: **Halt! Stop! Stop!** *(SERGEANT again walks*
35   *over to LITTLE ONE, who is very focused on his or her*

1   *shoes and doesn't notice SERGEANT.)*

2   **SERGEANT:** **What are you doing now, Little One?**

3   **LITTLE ONE:** *(Looking up at SERGEANT)* **Oh, hey there,**
4   **Sarge! I was just fixing my shoelaces. We were doing**
5   **that two-by-two marching — which I enjoyed very**
6   **much, by the way — and I noticed that my shoelaces**
7   **had come untied. Well, everyone knows that loose**
8   **shoelaces can cause tripping and stumbling**
9   **accidents, so I thought I had better take care of it**
10   **right away. Just hang on. I'm almost done.**

11   **SERGEANT:** *(Trying to keep from blowing up)* **You're**
12   **almost done, are you?**

13   **LITTLE ONE: Yep. Just one more thing.** *(Recites.)* **The**
14   **rabbit goes around the tree and into the hole, pull,**
15   **and there you have it! All tight and secure.** *(Stands up*
16   *and shakes a foot a few times to make sure the knot is*
17   *secure.)* **That's much better. Now, where were we,**
18   **Sarge?**

19   **SERGEANT: Where were we? Where were we?** *(Starts to*
20   *fume.)* **We were marching two by two until you**
21   **stopped to tie your shoe. You completely destroyed**
22   **the rhythm! We can't just jump back into it.** *(Gets*
23   *more and more upset.)* **All right, recruits! Not one by**
24   **one. Not two by two.** *But three by three!* **Now, go, go,**
25   **go!** *(The ANT RECRUITS scramble once again into a*
26   *new formation. This time they stand in lines, three by*
27   *three, and begin to march around the stage, faster this*
28   *time.)* **Hup-two-three-four. Hup-two-three-four. Hup-**
29   **two-three-four. Hup-two-three-four. The ants go**
30   **marching three by three.**

31   **ANT RECRUITS: Hurrah! Hurrah!**

32   **SERGEANT: The ants go marching three by three.**

33   **ANT RECRUITS: Hurrah! Hurrah!**

34   **SERGEANT: The ants go marching three by three ...** *(Stops,*
35   *turns around, and stares in disbelief. LITTLE ONE has*

1   *wandered off to one side of the stage and is trying to*
2   *climb something.)* **Halt! Stop!** *(ANT RECRUITS once*
3   *again stumble to a halt. SERGEANT crosses to LITTLE*
4   *ONE.)* **Little One! What do you think you are doing**
5   **now?**
6   **LITTLE ONE: Oh, hey there, Sarge. Are we finally taking a**
7   **break?**
8   **SERGEANT: No we're not taking a break! Why did you stop**
9   **this time? You are supposed to be marching three by**
10   **three.**
11   **LITTLE ONE: Well, I was marching three by three, which**
12   **was quite a challenge, I tell you, when we passed this**
13   **amazing tree, and I just had to stop and climb it. I'm**
14   **sure you understand. Could you give me a lift?** *(Raises*
15   *a foot in the air and waits for a hand up from*
16   *SERGEANT.)*
17   **SERGEANT:** *(In a low voice)* **I have tried to be patient with**
18   **you, Little One. I didn't go ballistic when you stopped**
19   **to suck your thumb. I was even willing to wait while**
20   **you tied your shoe. But climbing a tree?** *This is going*
21   *too far!*
22   **LITTLE ONE: But, Sarge —**
23   **SERGEANT:** *(Reaching his breaking point)* **No, that's it! No**
24   **tree climbing! That's where I draw the line. Now, get**
25   **back over there and march. Hup-two. Hup-two. Left-**
26   **right. Left-right.** *(LITTLE ONE starts marching around*
27   *frantically. The ANT RECRUITS line up across the back*
28   *of the stage. LITTLE ONE marches in and around the*
29   *ANT RECRUITS as SERGEANT shouts out instructions.*
30   *Soon LITTLE ONE's marching starts to look more like*
31   *dance moves. He or she dances around the stage to the*
32   *SERGEANT's commands. Gradually, all the ANT*
33   *RECRUITS are dancing.)* **Stop! Stop! Halt! What are**
34   **you doing?**
35   **LITTLE ONE: We're dancing, Sarge. Come on. Try it. This**

1   is so much better than marching. Marching is
2   overrated. It's all the same. Dancing, on the other
3   hand, is creative and fun. You can move your whole
4   body, not just your feet. You can express your
5   individuality. *(Demonstrates with some unique*
6   *moves.)* Hey, look, it's starting to rain. We must be
7   doing a rain dance. Come on, Sarge. Get your groove
8   on. *(LITTLE ONE starts to sing a hip-hop version of*
9   *"The Ants Go Marching." One of the ANT RECRUITS*
10   *makes beat-box sounds with his or her hands and*
11   *mouth as accompaniment. Even SERGEANT gives in*
12   *and decides to dance.)*
13   SERGEANT: Come on, recruits. Let's go! Down to the
14   ground to get out of the rain!
15   LITTLE ONE: *(Rhythmically)* The ants go marching one by
16   one.
17   ANT RECRUITS: Hoorah! Hoorah!
18   LITTLE ONE: The ants go marching one by one.
19   ANT RECRUITS: Hoorah! Hoorah!
20   LITTLE ONE: The ants go marching one by one.
21   ANT RECRUITS: The little one stopped to suck his thumb!
22   ALL: And they all went marching down. To the ground. To
23   get out of the rain. Boom, boom, boom, boom. I said,
24   "Boom, boom, boom, boom." I said, "Boom, boom,
25   boom, boom." *(ALL exit the stage, singing and dancing*
26   *as they go. Curtain.)*
27
28
29   Reference – Song:
30   "The Ants Go Marching One by One"

13. He Called for His Fiddlers ... Two?

Cast of Characters:

KING'S ASSISTANT, a very businesslike person in charge of seeing that the King gets what he wants when he calls for it.

PIPE HOLDER, a person in charge of the King's pipe.

BOWL CARRIER, a person in charge of the King's bowl.

FIDDLER 1, an accomplished fiddler.

FIDDLER 2, a second accomplished fiddler.

OLD KING COLE, the one and only merry old soul.

Props:

Two trays, pipe, bowl, clipboard, large scarf, and place a few chairs On-stage.

Scene:

A common room in Old King Cole's palace.

1   *(The PIPE HOLDER and the BOWL CARRIER are seen On-*
2   *stage, sitting and waiting patiently to be called for by OLD*
3   *KING COLE. FIDDLER 1 enters out of breath and checks*
4   *his watch. He sees that the PIPE HOLDER and the BOWL*
5   *CARRIER are still waiting and breathes a sigh of relief.)*
6   **FIDDLER 1: Whew! I thought I was going to be late.**
7   *(FIDDLER 2 rushes onto the stage, also out of breath. He*
8   *sees FIDDLER 1 and crosses to him quickly.)*
9   **FIDDLER 2: I made it! Boy, that traffic was a mess.**
10   **FIDDLER 1: You're telling me! It took over an hour to get**
11   **here. But the King hasn't called in the Pipe Holder or**
12   **the Bowl Carrier yet, so we still have some time.**
13   **Where's John?**
14   **FIDDLER 2: I don't know. I thought he was coming with you.**
15   **FIDDLER 1: No! I thought he was coming with you!**

1   **FIDDLER 2: He must be taking the bus.**

2   **FIDDLER 1: But he has all the equipment. He has our**
3   **fiddles. We can't perform with just two of us and no**
4   **fiddles.**

5   **FIDDLER 2: What are we going to do? I told you we**
6   **shouldn't let John be responsible for the fiddles. He's**
7   **unreliable!**

8   **FIDDLER 1: You told me? What are you talking about? *I***
9   **told *you* we shouldn't let John be in charge of the**
10 **fiddles!**

11 **FIDDLER 2: What are we going to do?** *(Starts breathing*
12 *heavily.)*

13 **FIDDLER 1: Now, don't panic. I'm sure he'll be here any**
14 **minute.** *(The KING'S ASSISTANT enters with clipboard*
15 *in hand.)*

16 **KING'S ASSISTANT: The King has called for his pipe.** *(The*
17 *PIPE HOLDER stands, holds a tray with the pipe up*
18 *high in a royal manner, and follows the KING'S*
19 *ASSISTANT Off-stage.)*

20 **FIDDLER 2: Oh, no! He's called for his pipe. We don't have**
21 **much time.**

22 **FIDDLER 1: Now, come on. It's just his pipe. We have**
23 **plenty of time.**

24 **FIDDLER 2: Maybe we should call John.**

25 **FIDDLER 1: How do you suggest we do that?**

26 **FIDDLER 2: I don't know.** *(Stops and considers this for a*
27 *moment, then starts calling out loudly.)* **John! John!**
28 ***John!***

29 **FIDDLER 1: Will you stop that? He's not going to hear you.**

30 **KING'S ASSISTANT:** *(Rushes On-stage.)* **What's all the**
31 **racket out here? The King is getting very upset. Bowl**
32 **Carrier, you're up! He's calling for you.** *(The BOWL*
33 *CARRIER crosses to the same exit as the PIPE HOLDER.*
34 *The KING'S ASSISTANT starts to follow. FIDDLER 2*
35 *stops him or her.)*

1 FIDDLER 1: Oh, excuse me, sir.
2 KING'S ASSISTANT: *(Turning back to FIDDLER 2, speaks*
3   *dryly.)* Yes?
4 FIDDLER 1: We have a little problem. You see, we are the
5   fiddlers here to play for Old King Cole.
6 KING'S ASSISTANT: Yes, you're up next. You'd better get
7   ready.
8 FIDDLER 2: Well, you see, it's actually kind of funny, but
9   there are only two of us here. Our third fiddler hasn't
10   gotten here yet.
11 KING'S ASSISTANT: So? *(FIDDLER 2 and FIDDLER 1 start*
12   *to laugh, trying to make light of the situation.)*
13 FIDDLER 1: Well, we can't play because our third fiddler
14   has all our fiddles.
15 FIDDLER 2: And he isn't here yet. So, you see, we are
16   fiddle-less. *(The FIDDLERS laugh again. The KING'S*
17   *ASSISTANT is not laughing with them.)*
18 FIDDLER 1: Do you think the King would be willing to
19   wait a few minutes until our third fiddler gets here
20   with the instruments? *(The KING'S ASSISTANT starts*
21   *to snicker.)*
22 KING'S ASSISTANT: Let me ask you something. Do you
23   know what would happen to me if the pipe did not
24   arrive when the King calls? *(Drags a hand across his or*
25   *her neck and makes a chopping sound to indicate that*
26   *he or she would lose his or her head.)* Do you know
27   what would happen if the bowl did not arrive when
28   the King calls? *(Again drags a hand across his or her*
29   *neck and makes a chopping sound.)* Do you know what
30   will happen to you if the entertainment does not
31   arrive when the King calls? *(FIDDLER 1 and FIDDLER*
32   *2 drag their hands across their necks and make*
33   *chopping sounds as if to indicate that they would lose*
34   *their heads.)* Very good! You are quick learners. I'll be
35   back for you in a minute, and you had better have

77

1   some entertainment for the King. People think he's a
2   merry old soul, but that's just his public face. Wait 'til
3   you see his private face! *(Exits.)*
4   **FIDDLER 2:** *(Starts to pace frantically.)* **What are we going**
5   **to do? What are we going to do?**
6   **FIDDLER 1: Calm down! We have to think. What else can**
7   **we do besides play fiddle music?**
8   **FIDDLER 2:** *(Panicking)* **Nothing! I can't do anything**
9   **except fiddle. I have no talent except fiddling!**
10   **FIDDLER 1: Oh, come now. Between the two of us, we**
11   **must be able to do something entertaining. We just**
12   **have to think.**
13   **OLD KING COLE:** *(From Off-stage)* **Where are my fiddlers?**
14   **I want my fiddlers!**
15   **FIDDLER 2:** *(Running around frantically)* **He's coming. The**
16   **King is coming! And we're going to be ...** *(Makes the*
17   *cutting noise and motion on his neck.)*
18   **FIDDLER 1: Now, don't lose your head!**
19   **OLD KING COLE:** *(Enters gruffly, carrying his pipe and*
20   *bowl, followed by the KING'S ASSISTANT.)* **Play for me,**
21   **fiddlers! I want to be entertained.** *(OLD KING COLE*
22   *takes a seat On-stage. The KING'S ASSISTANT stands*
23   *next to him with a serving tray. OLD KING COLE sets*
24   *his pipe and bowl on the serving tray. The two*
25   *FIDDLERS look at each other and walk forward*
26   *tentatively.)*
27   **FIDDLER 1: Well, your honor, uh, your majesty, uh, your**
28   **royal highest-ness.** *(Bows deeply. FIDDLER 2 follows*
29   *his lead and bows as well. FIDDLER 1 starts winging it.)*
30   **We thought we'd do a little something different for**
31   **you tonight.**
32   **FIDDLER 2: That's right. We want to do something a little**
33   **different for you tonight.**
34   **OLD KING COLE:** *(Suspiciously)* **Like what?**
35   **FIDDLER 1:** *(Stalling)* **Well, we thought we'd let you**

1   choose.

2   **FIDDLER 2: That's right! You choose.**

3   **OLD KING COLE: Me, choose? Well, that's novel. All right.**

4   *(Thinks about it then comes up with an idea.)* **I would**

5   **like to hear you recite.**

6   **FIDDLER 2: Recite?**

7   **OLD KING COLE: Yes, recite.** *(Leans forward.)* **You can**

8   **recite, can't you?**

9   **FIDDLER 1: Of course we can recite. We love to recite. Is**

10   **there anything in particular you'd like to hear?**

11   **OLD KING COLE: Hmmmm. What about something from**

12   **Shakespeare's *Romeo and Juliet!***

13   **FIDDLER 1: *Romeo and Juliet?***

14   **FIDDLER 2: *Romeo and Juliet?***

15   **OLD KING COLE:** *(Giving them the evil eye)* **You do know**

16   ***Romeo and Juliet,* don't you?**

17   **FIDDLER 1: Of course we know *Romeo and Juliet*. Who**

18   **doesn't know *Romeo and Juliet?*** *(FIDDLER 2 nudges*

19   *FIDDLER 1 and whispers toward him.)*

20   **FIDDLER 2: I don't know *Romeo and Juliet!*** *(FIDDLER 1*

21   *whispers back to FIDDLER 2.)*

22   **FIDDLER 1: Just follow my lead.** *(FIDDLER 1 grabs a large*

23   *scarf that is sitting on a nearby chair and covers his*

24   *head to dress as Juliet. He steps up on a sturdy chair*

25   *and begins to recite.)* **O, Romeo! Romeo! Wherefore**

26   **art thou, Romeo? Deny thy father and refuse thy**

27   **name. Or, if thou wilt not, be but sworn my love, and**

28   **I'll no longer be a Capulet.**

29   **FIDDLER 2:** *(Starts to clap.)* **Oh, that was marvelous! I had**

30   **no idea you could act.**

31   **FIDDLER 1:** *(Aside to FIDDLER 2)* **Stop clapping and start**

32   **playing Romeo.**

33   **FIDDLER 2: Oh, OK.** *(Stands below FIDDLER 1's chair and*

34   *thinks a moment.)* **Hey, Juliet. It's me, your Romeo!**

35   **Down here. Come on down! Let's go out and get**

1   **something to eat, maybe catch a movie.**

2   **FIDDLER 1:** *(Aside to FIDDLER 2)* **That's not how it goes!**

3   **FIDDLER 2: I told you, I don't know the play. I'm making**

4   **it up.**

5   **FIDDLER 1: No kidding.** *(Jumps down off the chair.)* **O**

6   **where, O where is my Romeo? O look. He is dead.**

7   **FIDDLER 2:** *(Whispers to FIDDLER 1.)* **I am?**

8   **FIDDLER 1:** *(Whispers back to FIDDLER 2.)* **You are.**

9   *(FIDDLER 2 drops to the floor. FIDDLER 1 kneels next to*

10   *him.)* **O, my sweet Romeo! I shall be brief. O happy**

11   **dagger, this is thy sheath.** *(FIDDLER 1 stabs himself*

12   *with an imaginary knife. To the knife)* **There rust and**

13   **let me die.** *(FIDDLER 1 dies dramatically and collapses*

14   *across FIDDLER 2. They lie there for a moment, then*

15   *jump to their feet and take a few bows.)*

16 **OLD KING COLE:** *(Claps, but is confused at what he has*

17   *seen.)* **I don't remember the story going quite like**

18   **that.**

19 **FIDDLER 1: Well, that was the new, revised version. It's**

20   **just recently been released.**

21 **OLD KING COLE: Hmmmm. I think I prefer the old**

22   **version.**

23 **FIDDLER 2: Well, to each his own. Thanks for coming, and**

24   **we'll see you next time you call.** *(The FIDDLERS start*

25   *to leave. OLD KING COLE stands and roars.)*

26 **OLD KING COLE: Come back here! I still want to be**

27   **entertained!** *(Comes up with a new idea.)* **What about**

28   **some opera?**

29 **FIDDLER 1: Oh no, we couldn't do opera. We don't know**

30   **any ...** *(The KING'S ASSISTANT is standing behind OLD*

31   *KING COLE, making the throat-chopping motion*

32   *toward the FIDDLERS. They both swallow deeply.*

33   *FIDDLER 1 continues.)* **Opera is our favorite! Isn't it?**

34   *(Nudges FIDDLER 2.)* **In fact, my friend here is an**

35   **amazing opera singer.** *(Puts his hand on FIDDLER 2's*

1   *shoulder and pats him solidly.)*

2   **OLD KING COLE: He is?**

3   **FIDDLER 2:** *(To FIDDLER 1)* **I am?**

4   **FIDDLER 1: Now, don't be so modest, friend. Come on,**

5   **now. Sing for the King. Sing your favorite aria. I'll**

6   **back you up.** *(Smiles broadly at FIDDLER 2, whose eyes*

7   *have grown very big. During the following "aria," the*

8   *two FIDDLERS ad-lib their own melodic version of an*

9   *opera aria.* [Author's Note: There is no wrong or right

10   way to sing this aria, so have fun.] *)*

11   **FIDDLER 2:** *(He clears his throat, clasps his hands in front*

12   *of his chest, and starts to sing, making it up all the way.*

13   *All the following aria lines are sung.)* **Oh, my heart is**

14   **weary and cold.**

15   **FIDDLER1:** *(Sings a response to FIDDLER 2.)* **Weary and**

16   **cold.**

17   **FIDDLER 2:** *(Singing)* **And I don't know where I'm going.**

18   **FIDDLER 1:** *(Echoing again)* **Where am I going?**

19   **FIDDLER 2:** *(Gaining courage and becoming more dramatic*

20   *as he continues)* **The leaves are falling around me.**

21   **Round and round about me.**

22   **FIDDLER 1:** *(Singing again)* **Round and round. Round and**

23   **round.**

24   **FIDDLER 2:** *(Even more dramatically)* **I must go ... and find**

25   **my love.**

26   **FIDDLER 1:** *(Echoing)* **Where is your love? Where is your**

27   **love?** *(The two FIDDLERS continue to sing the*

28   *following lines.)*

29   **FIDDLER 2: My love, my love is gone!**

30   **FIDDLER 1: Your love is gone! Your love is gone!**

31   **FIDDLER 2: I shall sail across the ocean.**

32   **FIDDLER 1: He shall sail. He shall sail.**

33   **FIDDLER 2: I shall sail across the sea.**

34   **FIDDLER 1: He shall sail. He shall sail.**

35   **FIDDLER 2:** *(The big finale)* **And ... I ... shall ... never ...**

1   *return!*

2   **FIDDLER 1:** *(Echoing FIDDLER 2.)* **Never return!** *(The*

3   *FIDDLERS end the aria dramatically with their arms in*

4   *the air. OLD KING COLE stands and applauds. He is*

5   *obviously moved by their performance.)*

6   **OLD KING COLE: Bravo! Bravo! That aria was fantastic!**

7   **What talent! You moved me to tears. I want you two to**

8   **come back tomorrow night and perform an entire**

9   **opera for me, from beginning to end. And I'm going**

10   **to invite some friends! We'll make a party out of it. A**

11   **huge party!**

12   **FIDDLER 2: Oh, but we can't ...** *(The KING'S ASSISTANT*

13   *makes the motion on his or her neck again. The*

14   *FIDDLERS force smiles.)*

15   **FIDDLER 1:** *(Finishing FIDDLER 2's sentence.)* **Wait! We**

16   **can't wait! We will be here tomorrow night to**

17   **perform for you again. Maybe something in Italian**

18   **next time.**

19   **OLD KING COLE: Marvelous! I** *love* **Italian opera! We'll**

20   **serve pasta and pepperoni pizza. It will be a theme**

21   **party. Until tomorrow night, my friends. Ta-ta!** *(OLD*

22   *KING COLE exits humming the aria the FIDDLERS*

23   *have just sung. The KING'S ASSISTANT follows OLD*

24   *KING COLE out. He or she looks back at the FIDDLERS*

25   *and smiles, giving them two thumbs up. The two*

26   *FIDDLERS look at each other, fear-stricken. Both make*

27   *the head-chopping hand motion on their necks again.*

28   *Curtain.)*

29

30

31   **Reference – Nursery Rhyme:**

32   "Old King Cole was a merry old soul

33   And a merry old soul was he.

34   He called for his pipe and he called for his bowl,

35   And he called for his fiddlers three."

14. A Party to Die For

Cast of Characters:

PARTY PLANNER, a very enthusiastic professional, hoping to make a name for himself or herself in the outrageous and exciting event-planning business.

BLACKBIRD 1, an irate blackbird.

BLACKBIRD 2, a second irate blackbird.

BLACKBIRD 3, a frightened blackbird.

BLACKBIRD 4, a delirious blackbird.

Props:

Clipboard with paper.

Scene:

Outside a palace where a huge gala birthday party for the King is taking place.

1   *(The four BLACKBIRDS enter in a panic. They are*
2   *apparently covered with something gooey. They are out*
3   *of breath and extremely upset. The BLACKBIRDS are*
4   *reacting to something traumatic that has just happened*
5   *to them Off-stage.)*
6   **BLACKBIRD 1: What was that? What just happened to us?**
7   *(The BLACKBIRDS look Off-stage in the direction they*
8   *have just entered. They try to wipe the sticky substance*
9   *from their wings. BLACKBIRDS 3 and 4 eventually*
10   *collapse to the ground.)*
11   **BLACKBIRD 2: I have no idea! We barely made it out with**
12   **our lives! How many are here?** *(Starts to count the others*
13   *On-stage.)* **One** − **two** − **three** − *(Points to himself or*
14   *herself.)* **and four. Where are the other twenty?**
15   **BLACKBIRD 3:** *(Shudders.)* **Maybe they didn't make it.**
16   **BLACKBIRD 4:** *(Wailing)* **Oh, no!** *(Covers face with arms.)*
17   **BLACKBIRD 1: Now settle down. Don't jump to conclusions.**

1   **BLACKBIRD 2:** That's right. I saw everybody swarm and
2   fly around the room when the pie was cut open. I
3   think everybody made it out alive.
4   **BLACKBIRD 4:** *(Wails again and swoons.)* **Ohhhh!**
5   **BLACKBIRD 1:** They probably just took off.
6   **BLACKBIRD 3:** Well, you can't blame them for that! We
7   should get out of here, too, before they stick us in
8   another pie. *(Gets up.)* Come on, let's go!
9   **BLACKBIRD 2:** Not so fast! We've got some unfinished
10   business with you-know-who!
11   **BLACKBIRD 4:** Who?
12   **BLACKBIRD 3:** Who?
13   **BLACKBIRD 1:** Who? *(PARTY PLANNER enters cheerfully.*
14   *He or she is carrying a clipboard and pencil and is in a*
15   *very jovial mood.)*
16   **PARTY PLANNER:** *(Very excited)* **Well done, everyone! Well**
17   **done! That was superb! And what a surprise! Now**
18   **that's what I call a main course! Did you see the look**
19   **on the Queen's face? Just before she fainted, I mean.**
20   **Fabulous! You have created quite a buzz. Quite a buzz**
21   **indeed! Let's see the French court top that at next**
22   **year's *carnival!*** *(Pronounces the word "carnival" with a*
23   *French accent.)*
24   **BLACKBIRD 2:** *You!* *(Points at the PARTY PLANNER and*
25   *walks slowly toward him or her.)* **You almost killed us!**
26   **PARTY PLANNER:** *(Backing up, innocently)* **What? What**
27   **are you talking about?**
28   **BLACKBIRD 1:** Don't act all innocent with us, buddy. What
29   were you thinking?
30   **PARTY PLANNER:** What do you mean "what was I
31   thinking?" I was thinking we were going to throw the
32   most amazing, most spectacular party the world has
33   ever seen. And we did just that! Listen. *(Runs to the*
34   *place from which the BLACKBIRDS entered and cups a*
35   *hand up to his or her ear.)* **You can still hear them**

1   cheering. They loved it. They just loved it! You all
2   were a hit!
3   BLACKBIRD 2: You nut! We were almost baked to death!
4   It's a miracle we got out of there with all our feathers
5   intact!
6   BLACKBIRD 4: *(Swoons again.)* Ooooh!
7   BLACKBIRD 3: You never told us we'd have to get baked!
8   We wouldn't have agreed to this whole thing if you
9   had mentioned anything about baking!
10 BLACKBIRD 4: That's right!
11 BLACKBIRD 1: That's right!
12 PARTY PLANNER: Well, we had to make it look
13   convincing. The King would have been suspicious if
14   we had brought out an unbaked pie, set it before
15   him, and asked him to cut into it.
16 BLACKBIRD 4: *(Swoons again.)* Ooooh.
17 PARTY PLANNER: *(Trying to explain to the BLACKBIRDS)*
18   It had to be a surprise. Don't you get it? We had to
19   brown the top of the crust a little. That's all. You
20   know, to give it that crispy, realistic look.
21 BLACKBIRD 2: Brown the top? *Brown the top?* It was a
22   hundred and fifty degrees in that pie! A hundred and
23   fifty degrees! And there was some kind of goo in
24   there, too!
25 BLACKBIRD 3: Yeah! Something warm and gooey that
26   stuck to our feathers and made it almost impossible
27   to fly away.
28 PARTY PLANNER: Oh, dear. That must have been the
29   sauce. Hmmmm. That probably wasn't a good idea,
30   was it?
31 BLACKBIRD 1: The sauce? There was sauce in that pie?
32 PARTY PLANNER: Well, yes, the recipe called for sauce.
33 BLACKBIRD 3: You used a recipe?
34 BLACKBIRD 2: *(Shocked)* What? Were you going to eat us?
35 BLACKBIRD 4: *(Swoons again.)* Ooooh.

1   **PARTY PLANNER:** *(Smiles unconvincingly.)* **No, of course**
2   **not. It was just a back-up plan. You know, in case**
3   **anything went wrong.** *(Recovering)* **But of course**
4   **nothing could go wrong, right? And nothing did go**
5   **wrong! The King cut the pie, and you all flew out to**
6   **the amazement of the entire crowd as they cheered,**
7   **fainted, and applauded. Although ...** *(Stops.)*
8   **BLACKBIRD 1: What? Although, what?**
9   **PARTY PLANNER:** *(Refers to the clipboard.)* **It's just that**
10   **according to your contract, you were supposed to**
11   **come out singing "Happy Birthday" to the King.** *(The*
12   *BLACKBIRDS start to complain bitterly. The following*
13   *dialogue happens simultaneously.)*
14   **BLACKBIRD 2: What are you talking about?**
15   **BLACKBIRD 1: You have got to be kidding!**
16   **BLACKBIRD 3: We were supposed to sing?**
17   **BLACKBIRD 4: We were flying for our lives!** *(PARTY*
18   *PLANNER stops them.)*
19   **PARTY PLANNER: Look. I am just stating what was in your**
20   **contract.** *(Starts to read from the contract on the*
21   *clipboard.)* **"Clause One: four and twenty blackbirds**
22   **will be baked in a pie."** *(Looks up.)* **You see, it actually**
23   **does say "baked in a pie."** *(The BLACKBIRDS glare at*
24   *PARTY PLANNER threateningly. PARTY PLANNER*
25   *waves it off.)* **OK, OK. I'm willing to overlook that part.**
26   *(Reads again.)* **"Clause Two: When the pie is opened,**
27   **the birds will begin to sing, with the ultimate goal of**
28   **setting a dainty dish before the King." For his**
29   **birthday, I might add. And you were going to sing**
30   **"Happy Birthday" as a big, spectacular finish. It's**
31   **right here in your contract.**
32   **BLACKBIRD 2:** *(Politely)* **May I see that contract?**
33   **PARTY PLANNER:** *(Takes off a sheet of paper and hands it to*
34   *BLACKBIRD 2.)* **Of course. I have your copy right here.**
35   **BLACKBIRD 2:** *(Takes the contract and reads it carefully.)*

1   Hmmmm. Oh, yes. I see. Look at that. Very well.
2   *(Slowly rips the contract into little pieces as the PARTY*
3   *PLANNER watches on.)* **That's what we think of your**
4   **contract!** *(The BLACKBIRDS start to exit*
5   *triumphantly.)*
6   **PARTY PLANNER:** *(Calling after them)* **Well, that's just**
7   **fine. I'll get some other birds to be the stars of my**
8   **next event! And we'll do a cake next time. That's**
9   **right. A giant, beautifully frosted cake, and I'll hire**
10   **some other birds to take your place, and they can get**
11   **all the glory. Like maybe some chickens! That's right.**
12   **I'll get some chickens to jump out of my cake and**
13   **sing for everyone.** *(The BLACKBIRDS stop and turn*
14   *back toward the PARTY PLANNER. They start to*
15   *snicker.)*
16   **BLACKBIRD 3: Chickens?**
17   **BLACKBIRD 4: Chickens?**
18   **BLACKBIRD 1:** *(Laughing)* **You're going to get chickens to**
19   **fly out of a cake as some big, flashy finale?**
20   **BLACKBIRD 2:** *(Laughing)* **Well, that will really be**
21   **something, considering the fact that chickens can't**
22   **fly.**
23   **BLACKBIRD 3: But they can jump.**
24   **BLACKBIRD 4: Yeah, they can jump up and down in the**
25   **cake.**
26   **BLACKBIRD 1: That would be hysterical! The top pops off**
27   **a cake and all you see is a bunch of chicken heads**
28   **bobbing up and down with those wiggly combs on**
29   **top as they try to claw their way out.** *(The*
30   *BLACKBIRDS are very amused at this idea.)*
31   **BLACKBIRD 4: Feathers would be flying!**
32   **BLACKBIRD 3: What a finale!** *(The BLACKBIRDS start to*
33   *imitate their idea of chickens bouncing up and down,*
34   *ineffectively flapping their wings as they try to get out*
35   *of a giant cake.)*

1   **BLACKBIRD 2: And what about their singing? Chickens**
2   **aren't exactly known for their beautiful voices, you**
3   **know.**
4   **BLACKBIRD 4: Squawking's more like it.** *(Starts to imitate*
5   *a chicken squawking. The BLACKBIRDS get carried*
6   *away with laughter as they all continue to mimic the*
7   *chickens, squawking and jumping up and down. The*
8   *PARTY PLANNER watches them. He or she is not*
9   *amused by their sarcasm.)*
10 **PARTY PLANNER: All right. Maybe chickens aren't the**
11   **best idea.** *(Thinks, and then gets a sinister look on his*
12   *or her face.)* **Perhaps I will have to go with warblers.**
13 *(The BLACKBIRDS freeze in their tracks.)*
14 **BLACKBIRD 1: What did you say?**
15 **PARTY PLANNER: I mean, if I really want to take this act**
16   **to the top, I should get some high-quality singers.**
17   **Don't you agree?** *(The BLACKBIRDS look at each with*
18   *concern.)*
19 **PARTY PLANNER: And I can't get any better singers than**
20   **warblers, can I?** *(Smiles at the BLACKBIRDS, looking*
21   *for a reaction.)* **I mean, you guys were OK for a trial**
22   **run. But when the heat was on, well, you sort of lost**
23   **your cool.**
24 **BLACKBIRD 3: What?**
25 **PARTY PLANNER: The fact is, you forgot to sing. You were**
26   **so worried about getting out of there alive that you**
27   **forgot to sing.**
28 **BLACKBIRD 2: Why, you!**
29 **PARTY PLANNER: And, let's face it. Blackbirds aren't**
30   **really known for their singing either. I mean, you**
31   **really only have one good song. Isn't that right? Don't**
32   **get me wrong, it's a good one. But, warblers!** *(Smiles.)*
33   **Now, warblers are real singers. Their song will bring**
34   **the house down.**
35 **BLACKBIRD 1: Now, wait a minute! You can't hire**

1   warblers. This is our gig.
2   BLACKBIRD 2: Yeah, this is our gig. We've got a contract!
3   *(The other BLACKBIRDS scramble to pick up the torn*
4   *contract and piece it back together.)*
5   PARTY PLANNER: *(Not listening to the BLACKBIRDS)* And
6   they can fly, too. Have you ever seen a flock of
7   warblers on a sunny day? They do loop-de-loops,
8   somersaults, and barrel rolls. Fantastic! They have
9   amazing versatility. I don't know why I didn't think
10   of this before.
11   BLACKBIRD 3: *(Holds up a few torn bits of the contract.)*
12   Look here. See? It says "four and twenty blackbirds."
13   Blackbirds! It says so right here in the contract!
14   PARTY PLANNER: *(Looking back at them)* Oh, you're right.
15   I'll have to write up a new contract and replace
16   blackbirds with warblers. Well, that's easy enough.
17   Thank you all for your help. It's been a pleasure
18   working with you! *(The PARTY PLANNER exits. The*
19   *BLACKBIRDS get up off the floor and look at each other*
20   *helplessly.)*
21   BLACKBIRD 1: *(Calling after the PARTY PLANNER)* But,
22   wait. Wait! We can sing!
23   BLACKBIRDS: *(Together)* We can sing! We can sing! *(The*
24   *BLACKBIRDS chase after the PARTY PLANNER,*
25   *singing "Happy Birthday" at the top of their lungs.*
26   *Curtain.)*
27
28
29   Reference — Nursery Rhyme:
30   "Sing a song of sixpence,
31   A pocketful of rye;
32   Four and twenty blackbirds baked in a pie.
33   When the pie was opened the birds began to sing;
34   Wasn't that a dainty dish to set before the King?"

15. E-I-E-I-Oh-No!

Cast of Characters:
FARMER, the famous "Old MacDonald" who had a farm and is
   now tired and old.
HORSE, ready to be put out to pasture.
PIG, enjoys his easy life, wallowing in the sty.
HEN, not putting out as many eggs as she was in her prime.
COW, too old to give milk, but still loves to graze in the fields.
ROOSTER, his "cock-a-doodle-doo" is not what it used to be.

Props:
Invitations for each animal and a handkerchief.

Scene:
Midmorning, in the barnyard of Old MacDonald's Farm. The
actors take on vocal and physical characteristics that express
their animal.

1　(HORSE enters first, holding an invitation he has
2　received from FARMER MacDonald. He looks around for
3　the other animals. They have not yet arrived. While he
4　waits, HORSE begins to reread his invitation silently,
5　mouthing the words. He is perplexed. PIG waddles in,
6　holding his invitation.)
7　**PIG: Hey, Horse! What's happening?** (The HORSE and PIG
8　exchange a complicated handshake. They have both lived
9　in the FARMER's barnyard for many years and are
10　showing signs of age.)
11　**HORSE:** (As they shake hands) **Pig, my friend. How goes it**
12　**this fine morning?**
13　**PIG:** (Puts one hand on his lower back, as if he is experiencing
14　some pain.) **Not too bad. My arthritis is acting up and I**
15　**have a new creak in my back, but all in all, I can't**
16　**complain.**

1 HORSE: I know what you mean. My trot's not what it used
2   to be either — achy knees. *(Leans over and rubs his*
3   *knees.)* It's this wet weather. It stiffens me right up.
4 PIG: I hear you. So, what's with this invitation from
5   Farmer MacDonald? *(Waves his invitation in the air.)* I
6   see you got one, too.
7 HORSE: I sure did and I can't figure it out. *(HORSE and*
8   *PIG read the invitation aloud together.)*
9 HORSE and PIG: "Dear Horse, Pig, Rooster, Hen, and Cow,
10   Please meet me first thing this morning in the
11   barnyard. I have something very important to talk to
12   you all about. Your old friend, Farmer MacDonald."
13 PIG: What do you think it's about?
14 HORSE: I have no idea. *(An idea comes to him.)* Maybe he's
15   building us a new barn!
16 PIG: Or maybe we're getting those new troughs we've
17   been wanting. *(ROOSTER and HEN enter. HEN is*
18   *badgering ROOSTER about the invitation she waves in*
19   *her hand. ROOSTER looks tired and weary.)*
20 HEN: Well, it could be something terrible!
21 ROOSTER: *(Unenthusiastically)* Yes, dear.
22 HEN: Maybe Farmer's upset about my ... *(Whispering to*
23   *ROOSTER)* egg production.
24 ROOSTER: *(Unenthusiastically)* I don't think so, dear.
25 HEN: But you know I don't lay as many eggs as I used to.
26   Maybe he wants to replace me!
27 ROOSTER: *(With the same tone of voice)* I wouldn't worry
28   about it, dear.
29 HORSE: *(Acknowledging ROOSTER politely)* Good
30   morning, Rooster. *(ROOSTER replies with an*
31   *unintelligible grunt.)*
32 PIG: *(Greets HEN.)* Mrs. Rooster.
33 HEN: *(Coldly)* Good morning, Pig. Horse.
34 HORSE: Hey, Rooster, I didn't hear any cock-a-doodle-doo-
35   ing this morning. What gives?

1 ROOSTER: Just a little sore throat, that's all. *(Tries to clear*
2   *his throat.)* **Nothing serious. I'm sure I'll be better**
3   **tomorrow.**
4 HORSE: Well, I hope so. I almost missed breakfast!
5 PIG: I, for one, appreciated the opportunity to sleep in and
6   just wallow for a change.
7 HEN: *(Finds PIG a bit disgusting.)* I've never noticed you
8   lack time for wallowing. In fact, you're always
9   wallowing. That's all you do!
10 PIG: What's that supposed to mean? I'm a pig! Pigs are
11   supposed to wallow. Besides, you do quite a bit of
12   sitting around yourself.
13 HEN: *(Miffed)* That's because I lay eggs! I have to sit to do
14   my job.
15 PIG: *(Nudges HORSE.)* Yeah? Well, I hear there aren't as
16   many eggs going to market these days. You know
17   what I mean? *(PIG and HORSE snicker to each other.)*
18 HEN: How dare you! There is nothing wrong with my egg
19   output. I am at the top of my game, I'll have you know.
20   I am in my prime. *(ROOSTER steps in to break up the*
21   *argument.)*
22 ROOSTER: All right, all right. That's enough of that. We
23   might as well admit that we've all seen better days.
24   None of us are in our prime anymore. But we've
25   nothing to be ashamed of. We've worked hard on this
26   farm all our lives. *(The ANIMALS grumble to*
27   *themselves. COW trots in slowly, waving her invitation.)*
28 COW: *(Cheerfully, with a sing-song tone)* Hello, everyone.
29   Am I late? I didn't hear the wake-up call. What's going
30   on? I received this invitation from Farmer
31   MacDonald first thing this morning.
32 HEN: We all got an invitation. That's why we're here. Why
33   do you suppose Farmer MacDonald wants to meet
34   with us?
35 COW: Maybe it's a party! Do you think it could be a party?

1   Oh, I just love parties!
2   **HORSE: Maybe it's his birthday. Has it been a year since**
3   **his birthday already?**
4   **PIG: Perhaps it's my birthday!** I hope he brings cake or pie
5   or cupcakes or –
6   **ROOSTER: Maybe it's our anniversary, and he wants to**
7   **congratulate us for a job well done. We have all been**
8   **faithful workers on the farm for a very long time.**
9   *(ALL the animals agree with ROOSTER.)*
10   **COW: Oh, I'm so excited. A party – for us!** *(The ANIMALS*
11   *begin to get very excited and talk amongst themselves.*
12   *They don't notice at first when FARMER enters the*
13   *scene.)*
14   **FARMER:** *(Clears his throat to get their attention.)* **Ahem.**
15   *(The ANIMALS look up to see him and start to cheer,*
16   *with comments like "There he is!" "It's the man of the*
17   *hour!" "Good ol' Farmer MacDonald." FARMER waves*
18   *his arms to settle them down.)* **Well, thank you for that**
19   **warm welcome, everyone. My goodness, you're all so**
20   **chipper this morning!** *(The ANIMALS laugh and smile*
21   *to each other, expectantly waiting for the big surprise.)*
22   **Now, I'm sure you're all curious about why I've**
23   **invited you here today. Well, I have a little surprise.**
24   *(The ANIMALS continue to smile and nudge each other,*
25   *certain they have figured out that the little surprise is a*
26   *party for them.)* **You have all been such wonderful**
27   **friends and helpers over the years. I couldn't have**
28   **run this farm without you. You have long provided**
29   **me with milk, cheese, and eggs, rides into town, and**
30   **so much more. You have been faithful and devoted**
31   **friends, and I appreciate you all so much.** *(The*
32   *ANIMALS pat each other on the back. They are feeling*
33   *so proud.)* **In fact, I have done so well with this farm**
34   **over the years, thanks to your hard work, that I have**
35   **decided ...** *(The ANIMALS lean in, expectantly.)* **I have**

1   decided to retire and move to Mexico. *(The ANIMALS*
2   *are shocked. They react as a group with lines such as*
3   *"What?" "Mexico?" "What did he say?" "You've got to be*
4   *kidding!" "Where's Mexico?" etc.)* **So, thank you from**
5   **the bottom of my heart, and a grateful good-bye to**
6   **everyone. I will be leaving the farm at the end of the**
7   **week. I know you will have no trouble finding new**
8   **homes. I will miss you all.** *(As if this is the last word,*
9   *FARMER waves and turns to leave. The ANIMALS*
10 *quickly look at each other, panic-stricken, then run and*
11 *stop him.)*
12 **HORSE: Whoa, whoa, whoa there, Farmer MacDonald. I**
13 **don't understand. We have been devoted to you!**
14 **PIG: That's right. Devoted!**
15 **HEN: We have lived our lives just to make you happy.** *(The*
16 *ANIMALS nod and agree with these statements.)*
17 **ROOSTER: We love you!**
18 **COW: That's right. We don't want to live anywhere else. We**
19 **need you and you need us!**
20 **FARMER: Correction. I did need you. But now you're old,**
21 **and farm work is getting difficult for you, and I'm old**
22 **and I don't want to work that hard either. So,** *(Pause)*
23 **I'm moving to Guadalajara. See ya!** *(FARMER turns to*
24 *exit again. The ANIMALS stop him once more.)*
25 **ROOSTER: But you can't just move to Mexico!**
26 **FARMER: I can't?**
27 **HEN: You certainly cannot. Who's going to feed us?**
28 **PIG: Yeah, who's going to feed us?**
29 **HORSE: And who's going to water us?**
30 **COW: Yes, who's going to water us?**
31 **ROOSTER:** *(Searching for another reason)* **And who's going**
32 **to sing that charming little "E-I-E-I-O" song with us?**
33 **It's your favorite. You wrote it just for us.** *(The*
34 *ANIMALS agree with ROOSTER.)*
35 **FARMER: You'll just have to sing that song by yourselves**

1   **from now on.** *(Stops. He is moved by their long faces.)*
2   **Look, there are plenty of other farms in the area. I'm**
3   **sure you can all find a nice, cozy place to live.**
4 **HORSE: But, we're** *old!* **You said so yourself. Nobody**
5   **wants a broken-down old horse with achy knees.**
6 **HEN:** *(Sadly)* **Or an unproductive hen.**
7 **ROOSTER: Or a rooster who can no longer crow.**
8   *(Demonstrates his pathetic "cock-a-doodle-doo," then*
9   *starts to tear up.)*
10 **PIG: Or a big, fat lazy pig!** *(ALL stop and look at PIG.)* **What?**
11 **COW: I don't think you'll have any trouble finding a place**
12   **to go, Pig.**
13 **PIG:** *(Naïvely)* **Really? I won't?**
14 **HEN: Certainly not. You'll make someone a nice holiday**
15   **ham or two.** *(PIG finally gets the picture. He screams*
16   *and hides behind HORSE.)*
17 **PIG: They'll never take me alive!**
18 **HORSE:** *(To FARMER)* **You don't want that to happen to**
19   **Pig, do you?** *(The ANIMALS fold their hands in a*
20   *begging position and look wide-eyed at FARMER.*
21   *FARMER considers the problem as the ANIMALS*
22   *slowly begin to sing.)*
23 **HORSE: "With a neigh, neigh here."**
24 **HEN: "And a brawck, brawck there."**
25 **COW: "Here a moo."**
26 **PIG: "There a snort."** *(They all sing together. FARMER is*
27   *noticeably moved.)*
28 **ANIMALS: "Everywhere a ..."**
29 **ROOSTER:** *(Lets out his strongest possible crow.)* **"Cock-a-**
30   **doodle-doo!"**
31 **ANIMALS:** *(Loudly)* **"Old MacDonald had a farm ..."**
32 **FARMER:** *(Blows his nose, then softly and slowly sings)* **"E-**
33   **I,"** *(Sniff)* **"E-I."** *(Sniffs again. The ANIMALS put their*
34   *arms around each other with FARMER in the middle.*
35   *They sing the last note together.)*

1   **ALL: "Ohhhh!"** *(There are hugs all around. Suddenly,*
2   *FARMER breaks out of the emotional scene.)*
3   **FARMER: All right, all right. That's enough of the**
4   **waterworks. Well ... why not? Why didn't I think of**
5   **this before? You can all come with me.** *(The ANIMALS*
6   *are shocked.)* **That's right. You can all come with me to**
7   **Mexico. Why not? We've been together this long. We**
8   **all deserve to retire. What do you say? We'll just**
9   **rewrite our little song to reflect our new home in**
10   **Mexico. So, start packing, everyone. We're heading**
11   *south!* *(The ANIMALS are overjoyed and begin to*
12   *celebrate with a new version of their song.)*
13   **ALL: "Old MacDonald had *una granja*,** *(Pronounced "gran-*
14   *ha")* **Ai-Yi-Ai-Yi-O! And on his granja he had *un gallo*,**
15   *(Pronounced "gah-yo." ROOSTER points to himself*
16   *happily.)* **Ai-Yi-Ai-Yi-O!"** *(ALL dance Off-stage with*
17   *newfound vigor and Spanish flair. Curtain.)*
18
19
20   **Reference – Song:**
21   "Old MacDonald Had a Farm"

16. The Twilight Realm

Cast of Characters:
NARRATOR, a mysterious "Rod Serling" type of character.
JACK SPRAT, the perfect husband, who can eat no fat.
EDITH SPRAT, Jack's contented wife, who can eat no lean.

Props:
Plates, silverware, glasses, napkins, remote control, and place a table and two chairs at Center Stage.

Scene:
Dinnertime at the Sprat home. The genre of this scene is reminiscent of *The Twilight Zone* television series, but for the purposes of this scene, we are visiting The Twilight Realm.

1 *(As the scene begins, JACK SPRAT and EDITH SPRAT are*
2 *sitting at their dinner table, having just finished their*
3 *evening meal. There are empty plates in front of them.*
4 *They are frozen in position as the NARRATOR enters. The*
5 *NARRATOR slowly surveys the scene, and then begins to*
6 *address the audience.)*
7 **NARRATOR: Ladies and gentlemen, for your consideration,**
8 **I present the portrait of a man and a woman, a**
9 **husband and wife by the names of Jack and Edith**
10 **Sprat. A contented couple, they find themselves**
11 **perpetually satisfied with their easy life and simple**
12 **routine. In a word, they are perfectly suited for life**
13 **together. Observe the husband, Jack Sprat.** *(The*
14 *NARRATOR walks around the table Upstage of JACK*
15 *SPRAT, who is still frozen in time.)* **Mr. Sprat is a simple**
16 **man, living a comfortable life at the side of his wife,**
17 **Edith. Strangely enough, they never argue, never**
18 **quarrel. They are completely symbiotic, interconnected,**
19 **and complementary to each other. For example, due to**

1   **some strange metabolic coincidence, Mr. Sprat can**
2   **eat only the tender lean on a cut of meat. His wife,**
3   **Edith, can eat only the fat of the meat. In this way,**
4   **they each get exactly what they want and never have**
5   **to share. But, this is only one small example of their**
6   **balanced relationship. In just a moment, the Sprats'**
7   **perfectly harmonious union will face its greatest**
8   **obstacle to date. Witness, if you will, a marriage put to**
9   **the ultimate test, here in ...** *(With intensity)* **The**
10   **Twilight Realm.** *(The NARRATOR walks to the side of*
11   *the stage, watching as the story unfolds. JACK SPRAT*
12   *and EDITH SPRAT come to life. JACK SPRAT stretches in*
13   *his chair, as if he has just eaten a deliciously filling*
14   *meal. EDITH SPRAT starts to gather the dishes.)*
15 **JACK SPRAT: My dear, that was delicious. Tender and**
16   **juicy and roasted to perfection!**
17 **EDITH SPRAT: Thank you, dear. I enjoyed it as well. The**
18   **fat was crispy and flavorful, just the way I like it.**
19 **JACK SPRAT: And did you get plenty of fat?**
20 **EDITH SPRAT: Absolutely, dear. Did you get plenty of**
21   **lean?**
22 **JACK SPRAT: I couldn't eat another bite.** *(The SPRATS*
23   *heave a big, satisfied sigh together.)*
24 **JACK SPRAT: Life together is so effortless, is it not, dear?**
25 **EDITH SPRAT: I agree wholeheartedly, dear. Our life**
26   **together is effortless.**
27 **JACK SPRAT: You can eat only the fat of the roast.**
28 **EDITH SPRAT: And you eat only the lean. You like to drive**
29   **the car to town.**
30 **JACK SPRAT: And you prefer to walk. I enjoy weeding the**
31   **garden.**
32 **EDITH SPRAT: And I prefer mowing the grass.**
33 **JACK SPRAT: I like to vacuum the house.**
34 **EDITH SPRAT: And I would much rather dust the**
35   **furniture.**

1   JACK SPRAT: I like to wash the dishes.

2   EDITH SPRAT: And I would much prefer to dry the dishes.

3   JACK SPRAT: I like to read the paper each morning.

4   EDITH SPRAT: And I like to listen to the radio.

5   JACK SPRAT: I can only sleep on the left side of the bed.

6   EDITH SPRAT: And I can only sleep on the right.

7   JACK SPRAT: It's a blessing, really.

8   EDITH SPRAT: The gift of a perfectly harmonious union.

9   *(The SPRATS smile contentedly toward the audience*

10   *and freeze as the NARRATOR walks back into the*

11   *scene.)*

12 NARRATOR: An unusually pretty picture, is it not? But

13   can the Sprats actually sustain their perpetual bliss?

14   Is there nothing on this earth that can upset their

15   seemingly perfect world? Something they are

16   unknowingly searching for, which is also searching

17   for them. Could there be a strange and distorted

18   object, seemingly insignificant, that sits at the

19   intersection of harmony and discord? A strange

20   intersection that resides in a shadow land called only

21   ... *(Intensely)* The Twilight Realm. *(The NARRATOR*

22   *slowly pulls an object out of a pocket and sets it on the*

23   *table in front of JACK and EDITH SPRAT. NARRATOR*

24   *then moves into the background of the scene as JACK*

25   *SPRAT and EDITH SPRAT come back to life.)*

26 JACK SPRAT: What do you say we watch a little television,

27   dear?

28 EDITH SPRAT: I think that would be lovely, dear. It's just

29   about time for the news. Would you turn on the telly

30   while I get the tea?

31 JACK SPRAT: My pleasure, dear. *(EDITH SPRAT takes the*

32   *dishes and exits toward the kitchen. JACK SPRAT gets*

33   *up, walks forward to their imaginary television, and*

34   *switches on the power. He returns to the table and as he*

35   *sits, he sees the strange object sitting on the table. It is*

1   *a remote control. He has never seen one before. He*
2   *looks at it with curiosity, poking at it carefully.)*
3   **JACK SPRAT: Why, what is this?** *(Looks at the object*
4   *intently. Then he calls to his wife.)* **Edith?** *(EDITH*
5   *SPRAT returns with the tea kettle.)*
6   **EDITH SPRAT: Yes, dear? What is it?**
7   **JACK SPRAT: Does this strange object belong to you?**
8   *(EDITH SPRAT examines the object as well.)*
9   **EDITH SPRAT: Why, no, dear. What is it? Where did it**
10   **come from?**
11 **JACK SPRAT: I have no idea. I've never seen it before. What**
12   **do you think it is?**
13 **EDITH SPRAT: I'm sure I don't know. Perhaps you should**
14   **pick it up.**
15 **JACK SPRAT: I don't know if we should touch it. It might**
16   **be dangerous.**
17 **EDITH SPRAT: What do you suppose all those buttons are**
18   **for?**
19 **JACK SPRAT: I have no idea. Perhaps it's an explosive of**
20   **some kind.**
21 **EDITH SPRAT:** *(Alarmed)* **An explosive? What would an**
22   **explosive be doing in our house? I think you should**
23   **pick it up and see what it is.**
24 **JACK SPRAT: Well, I think you should pick it up and see**
25   **what it is.** *(The SPRATS circle the table slowly with*
26   *their eyes glued on the object.)*
27 **EDITH SPRAT:** *(In a loud whisper)* **I think it's harmless. Go**
28   **ahead. Pick it up and see what it does.** *(JACK SPRAT*
29   *slowly reaches out and takes the remote, considering it*
30   *as he weighs it in his hand.)*
31 **EDITH SPRAT: Well, is it heavy?**
32 **JACK SPRAT: No, not too heavy.**
33 **EDITH SPRAT: Is it hot or cold?**
34 **JACK SPRAT: No, it's just room temperature.**
35 **EDITH SPRAT: Well, does it hurt your hand in any way?**

1   **JACK SPRAT:** *(Smiles. He is becoming quite comfortable*
2   *with the object.)* **No, it is actually quite comfortable in**
3   **my hand. Sort of like it was always meant to be there.**
4   *(Becomes mesmerized.)*
5   **EDITH SPRAT:** *(Reaches for the remote.)* **Well, maybe I**
6   **should try holding it for a while.** *(JACK SPRAT yanks*
7   *the remote away from EDITH SPRAT and in doing so,*
8   *accidently changes the channel on the television. They*
9   *both gasp with surprise.)*
10 **JACK SPRAT: What was that? Look! The channel has**
11 **changed on the television.**
12 **EDITH SPRAT: I don't like this, Jack. Put that thing down.**
13 ***Put it down!***
14 **JACK SPRAT: No, not yet. I want to try something.** *(Points*
15 *the remote at the television and starts pushing some*
16 *buttons. The television changes stations again and the*
17 *SPRATS jump with surprise.)* **Did you see that? I**
18 **touched these buttons on this strange object, and the**
19 **channel suddenly changed on the television. And**
20 **look – it's a football game. Well, that's nice, isn't it?**
21 **Perhaps we should just sit and have a look at who's**
22 **playing.** *(Sets the remote on the table and pulls up a*
23 *chair to watch the game. He is totally absorbed in the*
24 *show. EDITH SPRAT continues to look at the remote*
25 *with some skepticism. She finally gets up the nerve to*
26 *pick it up and points it at the television. The channel*
27 *changes again.)*
28 **EDITH SPRAT: Well, will you look at that? My favorite**
29 **cooking show is on.** *(EDITH SPRAT pulls up a chair,*
30 *next to JACK SPRAT, and begins watching her show.*
31 *JACK SPRAT is angered.)*
32 **JACK SPRAT: What do you think you're doing? I was**
33 **watching the game.**
34 **EDITH SPRAT: Yes, I know, dear. But I don't want to watch**
35 **the game. I want to watch my favorite cooking**

1   **program, and there it is.** *(JACK SPRAT looks around for*
2   *the remote. He crosses to the table but doesn't see it*
3   *there. He thinks EDITH SPRAT must be hiding it. He*
4   *walks slowly back toward EDITH SPRAT, looking over*
5   *her shoulder to see if he can locate the remote. He sees*
6   *it in her hand. Without warning he runs past her, grabs*
7   *the remote from her hand, and sits back in his chair,*
8   *pointing the remote at the television again. EDITH*
9   *SPRAT becomes miffed.)*
10 **EDITH SPRAT: I want to hold the strange object.**
11 **JACK SPRAT: No, I want to hold the strange object!**
12 **EDITH SPRAT: But you'll only turn on the football game**
13   **when I want to watch the food channel.**
14 **JACK SPRAT: That's right. If I hold the strange object, I am**
15   **in control of what station we watch. If you hold the**
16   **object, you will be in control of what station we**
17   **watch. And you will probably mute all the**
18   **commercials when I want to hear what they're**
19   **saying!**
20 **EDITH SPRAT: Why would you want to watch a commercial**
21   **for something you don't even need? Give me that**
22   **object!** *(Suddenly the SPRATS spring into action, trying to*
23   *wrestle the remote away from each other.)*
24 **JACK SPRAT: No, I want the object!**
25 **EDITH SPRAT: No, I want the object!**
26 **JACK SPRAT: Get your hands off it! It's mine!** *(The*
27   *NARRATOR claps his or her hands and the couple*
28   *freezes in their wrestling position. The NARRATOR*
29   *slowly walks forward and addresses the audience.)*
30 **NARRATOR: You have been traveling through another**
31   **dimension; a dimension not only of sight and sound,**
32   **but also the mind. A journey into a complex and**
33   **confusing world, where good and bad, right and**
34   **wrong, collide at catastrophic speed. Where perfect**
35   **harmony is only a thing that exists in the**

1   **imagination. Where Jack and Edith Sprat have**
2   **witnessed the sudden shattering of their perfectly**
3   **balanced relationship. You, my friends, have been**
4   **traveling through — The Twilight Realm.** *(Curtain.)*
5
6
7   **Reference — Nursery Rhyme:**
8   "Jack Sprat could eat no fat.
9   His wife could eat no lean.
10   And so between them both, you see,
11   They licked the platter clean."

17. A Home with a Sole

Cast of Characters:

MRS. SMITH, an old woman who lives in a shoe with a ton of children.

MR. JONES, a well-meaning real estate agent from the Really Friendly Real Estate Company.

CHILDREN, most of whom belong to Mrs. Smith.

NEIGHBOR KID, a straggler from one of last month's birthday parties.

PIZZA DELIVERY GUY, who decided to hang around and join in the fun.

Props:

Notebook, pen, and money.

Scene:

The front yard of the Smith home. The actors imagine and interact with an extremely large shoe standing Center Stage, which happens to be the old home of Mrs. Smith and her many children.

1   *(As the scene opens, several CHILDREN enter running*
2   *and playing as they circle the stage. MR. JONES enters*
3   *after them, reading from a notebook and looking for the*
4   *Smith home. The CHILDREN run around him, nearly*
5   *knocking him off balance. The CHILDREN run Off-stage*
6   *as MR. JONES recovers, brushing himself off. He sees the*
7   *"house," which is actually a huge, worn-out old shoe.*
8   *Surprised, he walks around to what would be the toe of*
9   *the shoe and examines it more closely as MRS. SMITH*
10   *enters from the heel of the shoe. She is surprised to see*
11   *MR. JONES looking at her house.)*
12 **MRS. SMITH:** *(Loudly)* **May I help you?**
13 **MR. JONES:** *(Startled)* **Oh! Hello. Are you by chance Mrs.**
14   **Smith?**

1   MRS. SMITH: That depends on who's asking.

2   MR. JONES: I'm terribly sorry. *(Reaches out his hand to*

3   *shake hers.)* My name is Mr. Jones. I'm from the

4   Really Friendly Real Estate Company. You called

5   about buying a house?

6   MRS. SMITH: *(Her mood changes instantly and she*

7   *becomes utterly delightful. She shakes MR. JONES'*

8   *hand.)* Oh, how do you do? Forgive my gruffness. You

9   can't be too careful with strangers these days.

10 MR. JONES: It's no problem. I quite understand. *(A group*

11   *of CHILDREN runs through, yelling loudly and waving*

12   *their arms. They circle MR. JONES and MRS. SMITH as*

13   *MRS. SMITH calls after them.)*

14 MRS. SMITH: Hey there! You children stop that. Can't you

15   see we have company? Go on. Go on. Get out of here!

16   *(Continues calling after the CHILDREN until they have*

17   *left the stage.)* I am so sorry, Mr. Jones. I'm afraid they

18   tend to forget their manners.

19 MR. JONES: Are all of those your children, Mrs. Smith?

20   There are so many of them.

21 MRS. SMITH: Oh, that's not all of them. There are many

22   more.

23 MR. JONES: My goodness! How many do you have?

24 MRS. SMITH: I'm not exactly sure. Fifteen? Twenty?

25   Thirty, perhaps? Once you get past ten, it's so hard to

26   keep track. *(Five or more CHILDREN run in again.*

27   *These can be the same CHILDREN as before or a*

28   *different group.)*

29 MRS. SMITH: Hold it! *(They stop in a line by MRS. SMITH.*

30   *She walks behind them, moving down the line as she*

31   *acknowledges each child.)* You see, Mr. Jones, this one

32   is mine. This one is mine. This one is mine. This one

33   is mine. This one is mine. *(She comes to the last child*

34   *in line and turns her around suddenly.)* And this one is

35   not mine! Who are you?

1 NEIGHBOR KID: I'm Jackie, ma'am, from next door.

2 MRS. SMITH: What are you doing here?

3 NEIGHBOR KID: I came for Joey's birthday party last
4   month and decided to stay.

5 MRS. SMITH: Aha! I thought there were more mouths
6   around here than usual. Don't you think your parents
7   are missing you?

8 NEIGHBOR KID: I never thought about it, ma'am. I've
9   been having too much fun.

10 MRS. SMITH: Well, the party's over, Jackie. Get your
11   goodie bag and head for home! *(The NEIGHBOR KID*
12   *runs off.)*

13 MRS. SMITH: *(Firmly)* And as for the rest of you, get back
14   to your chores! It's almost time for dinner. *(The*
15   *CHILDREN run off loudly, just as they entered.)*

16 MRS. SMITH: Pardon the interruption, Mr. Jones. Now,
17   where were we?

18 MR. JONES: Oh, yes — well, you contacted our office at the
19   Really Friendly Real Estate Company about buying a
20   new house.

21 MRS. SMITH: Yes, that's right. I think it's well past time to
22   get something bigger. We're bursting at the seams, so
23   to speak.

24 MR. JONES: I can imagine. *(Walks around the giant shoe*
25   *again.)*

26 MRS. SMITH: I thought the Really Friendly Real Estate
27   Company could help us find something suitable.
28   That's what you do, correct?

29 MR. JONES: Well, yes. We sell houses. But as far as I can
30   see, Mrs. Smith, this isn't really a house. This is a
31   giant shoe — a worn-out old boot, to be exact.

32 MRS. SMITH: *(Slightly offended)* Yes, it's an old shoe.
33   That's quite obvious. But it is also our home, and it
34   has been a wonderful place to live. It's simply too
35   small for us now, and we need something larger.

1　MR. JONES: I can see that, Mrs. Smith, but I don't sell
2　　　shoes. I sell houses. Now, if you'd like to move into a
3　　　nice two-story cottage or a ranch-style house, I might
4　　　be able to help. *(MRS. SMITH becomes distracted by*
5　　　*something on the roof and shouts up.)*
6　MRS. SMITH: Hey! You children get off that roof! I've told
7　　　you a million times! You may not rappel down with
8　　　the shoelaces! It's dangerous. Someday one will snap
9　　　in two and send you flying to the ground!
10　MR. JONES: They are adventurous creatures, aren't they?
11　　　How do you manage?
12　MRS. SMITH: As you can see, it's quite a challenge. A
13　　　bigger home would certainly help. Please, Mr. Jones,
14　　　I need your expertise. *(Another group of CHILDREN*
15　　　*runs through the scene, yelling wildly. There is a stray*
16　　　*at the end of the line, having as much fun as the rest. As*
17　　　*the CHILDREN run Off-stage, MRS. SMITH reaches out*
18　　　*and grabs the stranger by the arm.)* And who are you?
19　　　I've never seen you before. You can't be one of my
20　　　children.
21　PIZZA DELIVERY GUY: Oh, hi there. Pizza delivery for the
22　　　giant shoe. *(Holds out his hand to receive the money.)*
23　　　That'll be seventy-five dollars.
24　MRS. SMITH: *(Upset)* I didn't order any pizza.
25　PIZZA DELIVERY GUY: Well, someone did. That'll be
26　　　seventy-five dollars.
27　MRS. SMITH: I don't want any pizzas! Take them back!
28　PIZZA DELIVERY GUY: Too late. There's nothing left but
29　　　the crust.
30　MRS. SMITH: Get out of here!
31　PIZZA DELIVERY GUY: But my money!
32　MRS. SMITH: Get out!
33　MR. JONES: *(Reaches in his pocket and takes out money to*
34　　　*pay for the pizza.)* Mrs. Smith, please allow me. Here
35　　　you go, young man. I suggest you determine who's

1   doing the ordering next time, or you may not be as
2   **lucky.** *(The PIZZA DELIVERY GUY takes the money and*
3   *runs Off-stage.)*
4   **MRS. SMITH:** Thank you, Mr. Jones. You really didn't have
5   to. *(Starts to weep.)* I'm so sorry. It's just that I have so
6   many children. I don't know what to do with them
7   half the time.
8   **MR. JONES:** *(Feeling sorry for her)* It's all right, Mrs. Smith.
9   I'll see what I can do to help you get a bigger home.
10 I'm sure that will help. But I'm not making any
11 promises! *(Takes out his notebook and a pen.)* OK,
12 what do you need in a house?
13 **MRS. SMITH:** Thank you, Mr. Jones. Thank you. *(Recovers*
14 *from her crying and considers his question.)* Well, I
15 would like at least ten bedrooms, more if possible.
16 And eight bathrooms with several large bathtubs.
17 Make sure they're jetted. I want to be near the finest
18 schools in a nice, quiet neighborhood with no noisy
19 neighbors! I can't stand noisy neighbors! Did you get
20 that?
21 **MR. JONES:** *(Writes as fast as he can.)* Yes, Mrs. Smith, but,
22 eight bathrooms? I've never heard of such a thing.
23 **MRS. SMITH:** *(Ignores him.)* And a beautiful formal
24 entryway with a grand staircase, a fenced yard, and a
25 gourmet kitchen with a pantry. No laminate – that's a
26 deal-breaker.
27 **MR. JONES:** And how do you plan on purchasing such an
28 elaborate home, Mrs. Smith?
29 **MRS. SMITH:** Why, we'll sell this one, of course. Someone
30 will love this old shoe. It has character. You can
31 advertise it as a "vintage fixer-upper."
32 **MR. JONES:** But Mrs. Smith, this house is far more than a
33 fixer-upper. It's a total wreck! No offense, Mrs. Smith,
34 but this shoe has suffered years of abuse. No one in
35 their right mind would want to buy it. *(Motions to the*

1 *different areas on the shoe.)* **Look here. The sole is**
2 **splitting. The seams are ripping. The roof is leaking.**
3 **You said yourself that the shoelaces could break at**
4 **any moment.**
5 **MRS. SMITH: That reminds me, Mr. Jones. Our next house**
6 **must have Velcro instead of laces. Laces are so old**
7 **fashioned and dangerous. I want something more**
8 **modern this time and easy to clean, maybe a fancy**
9 **basketball shoe. It must be roomy like a nice, open-**
10 **concept clown shoe. But no gaudy colors! I prefer**
11 **earth tones, and I don't want to spend my time**
12 **renovating.** *(Starts to exit as she continues describing*
13 *her perfect house. MR. JONES shakes his head*
14 *hopelessly and follows her out. Her voice trails out as*
15 *she exits the stage.)* **The children must have a large**
16 **playroom, and there should be original hardwood**
17 **floors throughout. I think five or six thousand**
18 **square feet will suffice. What do you think?** *(Curtain.)*
19
20
21 **Reference — Nursery Rhyme:**
22 "There was an old woman who lived in a shoe.
23 She had so many children, she didn't know what to do.
24 She gave them some broth without any bread,
25 Then whipped them all soundly and put them to bed."

18. Once Upon a Quest

Cast of Characters:
PRINCE 1, the fearless and brave Prince brother.
PRINCE 2, the strong and brawny Prince brother.
PRINCE 3, the smart and studious Prince brother.
OFF-STAGE VOICES, a band of merry little people on their
  way home from work.

Props:
Two swords, magnifying glass, notepad, and pencil.

Scene:
Deep in a forest somewhere in "once upon a time" land.

1   *(PRINCE 1 springs onto the stage, full of vigor, with his*
2   *sword drawn, imaginary or otherwise. He surveys the*
3   *forest environment around him. PRINCE 2 bounds onto*
4   *the stage with his sword drawn and begins a playful*
5   *sword fight with PRINCE 1. After a few rounds of*
6   *swordplay, PRINCE 3 strolls On-stage. He is looking*
7   *through a magnifying glass, examining the flora and*
8   *fauna. He also carries a notepad and pencil with which he*
9   *jots down his observations. PRINCE 3 pays no attention to*
10 *the roughhousing of the other two. He is absorbed in his*
11 *own research. PRINCES 1 and 2 stop their swordfighting*
12 *and take in their surroundings.)*
13 **PRINCE 1:** *(Breathing deeply)* **Ah! Smell that, brothers — the**
14   **rich, deep aroma of the forest. My, how I've missed it!**
15   **We've been sitting around the castle for much too long.**
16   **It's good to be out in the fresh air again.**
17 **PRINCE 2:** *(Breathing deeply)* **You can say that again,**
18   **brother. The air is filled with the promise of adventure!**
19 **PRINCE 3:** *(Breathes deeply and analyzes the aroma.)* **My**
20   **olfactory nerves detect the molecules of decaying**

1   **wood, wet moss, lichen, and aging cedar —**
2   **specifically,** *(Sniffs again.)* ***Cedrela odorata,* if I'm not**
3   **mistaken. Hmmmm, interesting.** *Cedrela odorata*
4   **growing this far west? That's unusual. I had better**
5   **notate that for further investigation.** *(Writes in his*
6   *notebook.)*
7   **PRINCE 1: Oh, come now, brother. This is no time for**
8   **scientific study. We are on an exciting quest! And**
9   **what that quest will be, we have yet to see!** *(Tickled*
10   *with his wit)* **Hey, I made a rhyme!** *(PRINCE 1 and*
11   *PRINCE 2 laugh heartily. PRINCE 3 looks at a nearby*
12   *plant through his magnifying glass.)*
13 **PRINCE 3: Yes, well, you two can go off and have your fun,**
14   **but I am on a quest for knowledge!** *(Imitates the*
15   *vigorous laugh of the other two PRINCES, but his*
16   *attempt is pretty pathetic.)* **Just leave me alone and let**
17   **me find adventure in my own way.**
18 **PRINCE 2: But brother, we are all in this together.** *(Puts his*
19   *arm around PRINCE 3's shoulders.)* **We must share in**
20   **this adventure. All for one and one for all. We are**
21   **inseparable, just like the Three Musketeers.**
22 **PRINCE 1: That's right! We usually go on adventures**
23   **alone, but this time is different. This time we will**
24   **combine our princely powers on a quest to end all**
25   **quests! Hurrah!**
26 **PRINCE 2: Hurrah!** *(PRINCE 1 and PRINCE 2 look at*
27   *PRINCE 3 expectantly. PRINCE 3 considers this without*
28   *enthusiasm.)*
29 **PRINCE 3:** *(Gives in and puts away his notebook and*
30   *magnifying glass.)* **Oh, all right.** *(Weakly)* **Hurrah.**
31 **PRINCE 1:** *(Excited)* **Hurrah!**
32 **PRINCE 2:** *(Even more excited)* **Hurrah!** *(PRINCE 1 and 2*
33   *whip out their swords and begin vigorously fighting*
34   *again. PRINCE 3 attempts to stop them.)*
35 **PRINCE 3: Now, stop that! Stop that! If I can't take notes,**

1   **then you can't engage in swordplay. Now, put those**
2   **things away before someone gets hurt.** *(PRINCE 1 and*
3   *PRINCE 2 sadly put their swords back in their belts.)*
4 **PRINCE 3: That's better. Now, tell me, what exactly is our**
5   **quest?**
6 **PRINCE 1: I don't know.** *(Paints a word picture.)* **Maybe**
7   **we'll come across a fire-breathing dragon that is**
8   **holding a maiden captive in his dark, mountain lair.**
9 **PRINCE 3:** *(Considers this, then refers to it in Latin.)* **Ah! As**
10   **they say in Latin: the** *magna spirandi ignem draco.*
11   **That could be interesting.**
12 **PRINCE 2:** *(Paints a different word picture.)* **Or perhaps we**
13   **will find an evil witch who has locked a beautiful**
14   **maiden in an impenetrable tower.**
15 **PRINCE 3:** *(Responds with French.)* **Ah! The French refer to**
16   **it as,** *une tour impénétrable!*
17 **PRINCE 2: That's what I said — an impenetrable tower.**
18   **Why do you always have to overcomplicate things**
19   **with your French and Latin translations? Blah, blah,**
20   **blah.**
21 **PRINCE 3: Why do you always have to oversimplify things?**
22   **Can't you use your brain once in a while instead of**
23   **just using your brawn?** *(Does an exaggerated imitation*
24   *of PRINCE 2.)* **Duh, what's that mean? Duh, I don't get**
25   **it.**
26 **PRINCE 2: You're just jealous of my keen athletic prowess.**
27 **PRINCE 3: Jealous of you? I'd rather be smart than brawny**
28   **any day!**
29 **PRINCE 1: All right, you two. Stop your arguing. Brains are**
30   **good. Brawn is good. It depends on the situation.**
31   **We're going to need both on this quest, so try to get**
32   **along for once.**
33 **PRINCE 2: He started it!**
34 **PRINCE 3:** *(Under his breath, in Spanish this time)*
35   *Ignorante grande.*

1 PRINCE 2: What did he call me? Whatever it was, it
2   sounded bad! No fair calling me names in a language
3   I can't understand!
4 PRINCE 1: That's enough! Both of you, stop it! We have to
5   get on with our quest. OK, now let's see. Fire-
6   breathing dragons, impenetrable towers, what else
7   might we run into? *(Comes up with an unsettling*
8   *thought.)* I just thought of something. We might come
9   across the band of ruthless little humans that
10   inhabit these woods. *(PRINCE 2 and PRINCE 3 are*
11   *suddenly horrified.)*
12 PRINCE 3: *(Frightened)* You mean, the creatures the
13   Italians call the *persona piccolo?* There are *persona*
14   *piccolo* in these woods? Uh, maybe we'd better
15   rethink this quest.
16 PRINCE 2: *(Also frightened)* Yeah, I'm with him for once.
17   Fire-breathing dragons are one thing, but scary little
18   piccolo-whatever-he-saids are something else. Count
19   me out!
20 PRINCE 1: *(Trying to calm their fears)* I only said it was a
21   possibility. Look, I'm probably way off. In fact, I'm
22   sure there aren't any scary little humans in these
23   woods. I was thinking of a whole different forest —
24   not this one. Definitely not this one. *(PRINCE 1 tries to*
25   *laugh it off. PRINCE 2 and PRINCE 3 laugh weakly as*
26   *they look around with trepidation.)*
27 PRINCE 1: Now, look, we have to have a plan. What if we
28   come upon an evil witch? We have to know how to
29   talk to her so we aren't turned into frogs or stones or
30   something terrible like that.
31 PRINCE 2: Well, my strategy for talking with evil witches
32   is to lull them into a false sense of security. When I
33   speak, I use a wide variety of pitches. For example,
34   listen to how I use the full range of my voice when
35   approaching an evil witch. *(As he speaks the next*

1   lines, he exaggerates his voice to include very high
2   pitches and very low pitches. Switch back and forth
3   several times in the following dialogue.) "Hello,
4   **madam. How are you this fine morning? Me? Oh I am**
5   **just dandy, thank you. Did you happen to see a fire-**
6   **breathing dragon fly this way? I am on a quest to find**
7   **him and bring him down with my extremely strong**
8   **arm. You haven't seen him? Well, thank you so much**
9   **for your help. I shall now be on my way. Good day."**
10   **You see? By using my high and low tones, I have put**
11   **the witch off-guard and escaped without injury.**
12   **PRINCE 1:** *(Unenthusiastically claps for PRINCE 2.)* **Very**
13   **good, brother, very good. That will work well on the**
14   **occasional evil witch who is hard of hearing. I,**
15   **myself, have developed a technique that is infallible**
16   **when it comes to eluding evil witches.**
17   **PRINCE 2: Oh, really? Do tell.**
18   **PRINCE 1: Well, it goes like this. I use the pace of my**
19   **speaking to deter evil witches. Sometimes I speak**
20   **very rapidly. Then I confuse her by speaking very**
21   **slowly and deliberately. Fast — slow. Fast — slow. Let**
22   **me show you how it works.** *(Exhibits rapid speech*
23   *patterns followed by exaggerated slow patterns. Switch*
24   *back and forth several times during the following*
25   *dialogue.)* **"Hello, madam. How are you this fine**
26   **morning? Me? Oh I am just fine, thank you, so nice of**
27   **you to ask. Did you happen to see a fire-breathing**
28   **dragon fly this way? I am on a quest to find him and**
29   **bring him down with my extremely impressive bow**
30   **skills. You haven't seen him? Well, thank you so much**
31   **for your help. I shall now be on my way. Good day."**
32   **PRINCE 2:** *(Unenthusiastically claps for his brother.)* **Very**
33   **good, brother, very good. That will work particularly**
34   **well if we come upon an evil witch who has a short**
35   **attention span.**

1   PRINCE 3: And what if the evil witch is not an idiot, but
2   happens to be intelligent? Witches are known for
3   stirring up some complicated herbal concoctions,
4   you know. They know more about these woods than
5   you or I will ever know. I feel we should give the
6   witch the benefit of the doubt. Treat her respectfully
7   by using long pauses as we speak to encourage her
8   feedback. I would be glad to give you an example of
9   what I mean. *(Let the pauses create a unique way of*
10   *delivering the dialogue. Play with it. Fill the pauses*
11   *with thought. Use hands for emphasis during the*
12   *pauses.)* "Good morning, madam. How are you
13   *(Pause)* this fine morning? Me? Oh, I am *(Pause)* fine,
14   thank you, so nice of you to ask. *(Walks around*
15   *thoughtfully, considering what he is to say next.)* Did
16   you happen to see a fire-breathing dragon *(Pause)* fly
17   this way? I am on a quest *(Pause)* to find him and
18   bring him *(Pause)* down with my extremely sharp wit.
19   You *(Pause)* haven't seen him? Well *(Pause)* thank you
20   so much for your *(Pause)* help. I *(Pause)* shall now be
21   on my way. Good *(Pause)* day, madam." *(PRINCE 3*
22   *smiles, very satisfied with his performance. PRINCE 1*
23   *and PRINCE 2 look at PRINCE 3 in disbelief.)*
24   PRINCE 1: Well done, brother. That will be extremely
25   effective if we decide to put the evil witch to sleep.
26   PRINCE 2: By the time you get done talking to her, she will
27   have turned you into a frog, then a stone, then back
28   into a frog, and then a stone again!
29   PRINCE 3: What are you talking about? Pauses can be very
30   effective!
31   PRINCE 2: I think using the pitch of your voice is the most
32   effective technique!
33   PRINCE 1: And I think speaking with varied pace is the
34   only answer! *(The PRINCES continue to argue amongst*
35   *themselves. Suddenly, we hear some Off-stage*

1   *commotion. The PRINCES hear the noise and begin to*
2   *shush each other. They huddle together.)*
3   **PRINCE 2: Shhhh! Shhhh! Shhhh!**
4   **PRINCE 3: Shhhh! Listen!**
5   **PRINCE 1:** *(In a loud stage whisper)* **What was that?**
6   **PRINCE 2:** *(In a loud stage whisper)* **There's something in**
7   **the woods, and it's coming toward us.**
8   **PRINCE 3:** *(In a loud stage whisper)* **Maybe it's a fire-**
9   **breathing dragon.** *(The PRINCES listen again. Their*
10   *fear rises.)*
11 **PRINCE 2: Maybe it's an evil witch!** *(The PRINCES move a*
12   *little closer to the sound, clinging together in one big*
13   *huddle, listening intently. The noise continues to grow.*
14   *They begin to hear OFF-STAGE VOICES. Softly at first,*
15   *the voices grow louder, as if they come closer.)*
16 **PRINCE 1: Get ready, brothers. This is it. We have found**
17   **our quest. Or should I say our quest has found us!**
18   *(PRINCE 1 and PRINCE 2 slowly pull out their swords.*
19   *PRINCE 3 slowly pulls out his notebook and pencil.)*
20 **PRINCE 2: B-b-but, what is it?**
21 **PRINCE 3:** *(Paraphrase of Lady Macbeth)* **Screw your**
22   **courage to the sticking place, brothers, and we shall**
23   **not fail!** *(The OFF-STAGE VOICES are finally*
24   *recognizable.)*
25 **OFF-STAGE VOICES:** *(Singing)* **Heigh-ho, Heigh-ho, we**
26   **worked and now let's go.** *(Cheerful whistling follows*
27   *the singing. The PRINCES recognize the OFF-STAGE*
28   *VOICES as the dreaded little humans that inhabit the*
29   *woods.)*
30 **PRINCES:** *(Together in Latin)* ***Persona piccolo!*** **Run!** *(The*
31   *PRINCES panic, run around in circles, and exit away*
32   *from the voices, yelling and running at top speed.*
33   *Curtain.)*

1 **Reference — Fairy Tales:**
2 A mixture of princes from many stories.
3
4
5 **Author's Note:**
6 This scene introduces the actor's technique of using pace,
7 pitch, and pause to vary line delivery and make
8 presentations more interesting and ultimately, more
9 natural. This is an important tool for the student actor and
10 may be explored in other scenes and monologues as well.
11 You can also add the fourth "P" to the mix — projection.
12 Using a variety of loud and soft line deliveries adds interest
13 and brings out intent. Not all lines of dialogue are equal in
14 value, just as in our natural conversations. Using vocal
15 dynamics and emphasis makes it clear what is more
16 important and what is less important.

19. And the Winner Is ...

Cast of Characters:

MR. HARE, an extremely driven lop-eared rabbit.

MR. H'S ASSISTANT, in charge of keeping track of Mr. Hare.

MR. TORTOISE, a slow yet tenacious member of the Turtle family.

MR. T'S ASSISTANT, supports Mr. Tortoise.

REPORTER 1, represents KWAT-TV.

REPORTER 2, reports for the Sunnyvale Daily News.

REPORTER 3, reports for Radio KXAT.

Props:

Two podiums placed at Center Stage.

Scene:

The front steps of the Sunnyvale Courthouse.

1　(*The ASSISTANTS are getting things ready for a press*
2　*conference between MR. TORTOISE and MR. HARE. Both*
3　*are candidates for Mayor of the town of Sunnyvale. The*
4　*ASSISTANTS check their watches, as someone is obviously*
5　*late. There are two podiums facing the audience.*
6　*MR.TORTOISE stands behind one. MR. T'S ASSISTANT*
7　*stands next to him. The other is unoccupied. MR. H'S*
8　*ASSISTANT stands next to the unoccupied podium. The*
9　*REPORTERS are standing around waiting for the*
10　*questions to begin. It is clear by their reactions that it is*
11　*well past the scheduled time. When the scene begins, allow*
12　*a period of discomfort and disgruntled whispering before*
13　*the dialogue starts. Finally, REPORTER 1 speaks up.*)
14　**REPORTER 1:** (*Loudly*) **Excuse me. Are we going to get**
15　**started soon? This press conference was suppose to**
16　**start an hour ago!** (*EVERYONE grumbles in agreement.*
17　*MR. T'S ASSISTANT steps forward.*)

1 MR. T'S ASSISTANT: Perhaps Mr. Hare would like to
2   concede to Mr. Tortoise.
3 MR. H'S ASSISTANT: *(Nervous and slightly embarrassed)*
4   Of course not. Something important must have
5   happened to delay Mr. Hare. I just hope he hasn't had
6   an accident or something.
7 REPORTER 2: We can't wait around here all day.
8 REPORTER 3: That's right! If he's not here in two
9   minutes, we're going to interview Candidate Tortoise
10   without him.
11 MR. H'S ASSISTANT: *(Stalling)* Now there's no need to
12   rush to any decisions. I'm certain Mr. Hare will be
13   here shortly. I assure you, he is dedicated to this
14   election, and it is of the utmost importance for him
15   to be here today — *(All of a sudden there is a*
16   *commotion Off-stage and MR. HARE rushes in at top*
17   *speed. He stops Center Stage and pants heavily for a*
18   *moment before recovering. Then he jumps into*
19   *"candidate mode" and addresses the REPORTERS.)*
20 MR. HARE: My friends, it is my pleasure to be here with
21   you this fine day. Please forgive my tardiness.
22   Somehow, the time just got away from me. *(Crosses to*
23   *his place at the podium.)* Let the questioning begin!
24 MR. H'S ASSISTANT: Mr. Hare is now ready to answer
25   your questions.
26 MR. T'S ASSISTANT: And Mr. Tortoise, who has been
27   patiently waiting for Mr. Hare to arrive, is also ready
28   to address your questions.
29 MR. HARE: *(Turning to MR. TORTOISE)* Hey there,
30   slowpoke. How's it going? I haven't seen you around
31   for a while.
32 MR. TORTOISE: Good day, Hare. Still the last one to
33   arrive, I see.
34 MR. HARE: *(Defensively)* What's that supposed to mean?
35 REPORTER 1: Good morning, Mr. Hare and Mr. Tortoise.

1   **I am Reporter James from KWAT-TV. Perhaps you**
2   **could begin by telling the good people of Sunnyvale**
3   **why you want to be the mayor.**
4 **MR. HARE: Well, I think the good people of Sunnyvale**
5   **deserve only the best in their mayor. And since I am**
6   **the best, it is obvious they deserve me! Thank you!**
7   **Thank you!**
8 **REPORTER 1: And Mr. Tortoise, what is your answer to**
9   **that question?**
10 **MR. TORTOISE:** *(His delivery is slow and deliberate.)* **I will**
11   **do my very best to serve the people of beautiful**
12   **Sunnyvale, and to slowly but surely accomplish all**
13   **the goals and projects set forth by the people of this**
14   **fine town.**
15 **MR. HARE: Ha! Slowly but surely! Nobody wants their**
16   **mayor to move slowly but surely. When I am elected**
17   **mayor, I will get everything done in the blink of an**
18   **eye!** *(Looks to his right.)* **That's done!** *(Looks to his left.)*
19   **That's done! Just like that.**
20 **MR. TORTOISE: It doesn't do any good to do things**
21   **quickly if you don't do things well. I will do a good job**
22   **on every project I undertake, and eventually**
23   **everything will be finished and done well.** *(MR. HARE*
24   *snores as he pretends to be asleep at the podium. When*
25   *MR. TORTOISE finishes, MR. HARE perks up.)*
26 **MR. HARE: Boring!**
27 **REPORTER 2:** *(Introducing himself or herself)* **Reporter**
28   **Vanderbilt from the Sunnyvale Daily News. What**
29   **kind of a role model do you think you would be for**
30   **the young people of Sunnyvale? Mr. Hare?**
31 **MR. HARE: Well, it's quite obvious that adopting my**
32   **philosophy of life would be a huge benefit for the**
33   **young people of Sunnyvale. My philosophy is, "Just**
34   **do it — and do it as fast as you can! The faster the**
35   **better! Go, go, go! Faster, faster, faster! And then you**

1   have the rest of the day to kick back and have fun."
2   That's the way to your live!
3 REPORTER 2: I see. Mr. Tortoise, what kind of a role
4   model would you be for the young people of
5   Sunnyvale?
6 MR. TORTOISE: I believe I would be a very good role
7   model for the young people of Sunnyvale. My
8   philosophy is this: "Slow and steady wins the race.
9   Always take your time and do your best. Focus on the
10   task at hand, and don't allow yourself to get
11   distracted. When your work is finished, you will
12   know you have done your best."
13 REPORTER 3: *(Identifying himself or herself.)* Reporter
14   Smith from Radio KXAT. It seems you two candidates
15   are giving the voters a very clear choice. Is it true that
16   you gentlemen have been in competition with each
17   other before?
18 MR. HARE: *(Nervously)* No! It is not true! That is a vicious
19   lie. I have never seen this tortoise before in my life.
20   Next question, moving right along.
21 MR. TORTOISE: I don't know if you could call it a
22   competition. What do you think, Hare? It was really
23   more of an experiment.
24 MR. HARE: No, there was no experiment! There was no
25   competition! Mr. Tortoise is delusional. Make sure
26   you write that down in your notes. Candidate
27   Tortoise is delusional. Next question, please.
28 REPORTER 3: Mr. Tortoise, what do you mean by "an
29   experiment"? What kind of experiment was it? I'm
30   sure the listeners of KXAT Radio would be interested
31   to know.
32 MR. TORTOISE: Well, it was sort of a physics experiment.
33 MR. HARE: *(Getting louder)* What on earth does this have
34   to do with the election? *(Starts chanting.)* "Hare for
35   Mayor! Hare for Mayor! He can win with time to

1   spare!"
2   MR. TORTOISE: You see, Mr. Hare prides himself on being
3   as fast as the wind. He is certain he can succeed at
4   anything just by being the fastest. And he probably is
5   the swiftest runner I've ever seen.
6   MR. HARE: Why thank you, Tortoise. I am the fastest and
7   therefore, the finest candidate for the position of
8   Sunnyvale Mayor. Let's hear it for Hare! He'll get
9   every job done in no time flat. "Hare today – done
10   tomorrow!"
11 MR. TORTOISE: I, on the other hand, may not be swift ...
12 MR. HARE: Not swift? That's an understatement! He's so
13   slow he has to start cooking his dinner while he's still
14   eating his breakfast. *(Laughs at his own joke.)* He's so
15   slow he can't buy ice cream because it will melt
16   before he gets it home. *(Cracks himself up.)*
17 MR. TORTOISE: *(Unruffled by MR. HARE's jokes, picking*
18   *up where he left off)* As I was saying, I may not be fast,
19   but I am determined and consistent. I stay focused
20   and always finish the job. I am patient and
21   dependable. That is why I think I will be the best
22   mayor for the people of Sunnyvale.
23 REPORTER 1: But you still haven't told us what the
24   experiment was.
25 MR. HARE: *(Jumping in)* Oh, OK, look. It was just a little
26   fun and games to see who could get to the finish line
27   first. It was a joke!
28 MR. TORTOISE: And I wanted to prove that slow and
29   steady wins the race every time.
30 MR. HARE: That idea is so ridiculous we shouldn't even
31   bother talking about it. I am obviously the superior
32   runner between the two of us, and we ran a race. I let
33   him win so he could feel good about himself. I mean,
34   I even had to take a nap along the way in order to let
35   him win. It was crazy! End of story. Moving right

1   along. Who has the next question?

2   **REPORTER 2: So, let me get this straight. Mr. Tortoise**

3   **won a foot race against you, Mr. Hare?**

4   **MR. HARE: I told you, I let him win! Look, you want to see**

5   **who's faster? You want to see who's faster? I'll race**

6   **him again, right here and now, and I'll show you**

7   **who's faster! Ready, set, go!** *(MR. HARE runs past MR.*

8   *TORTOISE's podium and around toward the*

9   *REPORTERS. Throughout the next dialogue, MR.*

10   *HARE is continually distracted by one thing after*

11   *another. MR. TORTOISE slowly but surely follows after*

12   *him, around the podiums and through the*

13   *REPORTERS. MR. HARE doesn't notice that MR.*

14   *TORTOISE is passing him. MR. HARE stops at*

15   *REPORTER 1 and shakes his or her hand.)* **How do you**

16   **do? I am the famous Mr. Hare, running faster than**

17   **ever for Sunnyvale Mayor. Make sure you get my good**

18   **side.** *(Poses for the camera, then races a little farther to*

19   *REPORTER 2. MR. HARE leans an arm casually on*

20   *REPORTER 2's shoulder.)* **Question for you. There's a**

21   **group of one hundred rabbits. Ninety-nine take one**

22   **step back. What do you have?**

23   **REPORTER 2: I have no idea.**

24   **MR. HARE: A receding hare line!** *(Laughs uproariously and*

25   *turns as if addressing a crowd.)* **Thank you! Thank**

26   **you! I'll be here all week. Tell your friends!** *(MR.*

27   *HARE runs a little farther to REPORTER 3. All the*

28   *while, MR. TORTOISE, with focus and determination,*

29   *is very slowly running around the REPORTERS, back*

30   *toward the podiums. MR. HARE stops at REPORTER 3.)*

31   **So, do you know what a rabbit's favorite dance style**

32   **is?**

33   **REPORTER 3: I have no idea.**

34   **MR. HARE: Hip-hop!** *(Starts to break into a hip-hop dance,*

35   *showing off his best moves for the cameras. MR.*

1   *TORTOISE is focused on the finish line. Suddenly, MR.*
2   *HARE looks up from his routine and sees MR.*
3   *TORTOISE rounding the podiums.)* **Oh, no you don't!**
4   **Not again! Out of my way!** *(The entire scene changes to*
5   *slow motion. MR. HARE is scrambling for the finish*
6   *line. MR. TORTOISE is determined to get there first.*
7   *The REPORTERS are taking pictures and writing notes.*
8   *The ASSISTANTS are each cheering for their candidate*
9   *to win. The action is wild and crazy and all in slow*
10   *motion. The final frame shows MR. TORTOISE and MR.*
11   *HARE slowly reaching for the podium. MR. TORTOISE*
12   *wins by a hair. No pun intended. The action resumes at*
13   *normal speed. EVERYONE is panting from the exertion.*
14   *MR. HARE has ended up on the ground.)*
15 **MR. TORTOISE: And that is why I always say, "Slow and**
16   **steady wins the race."**
17 **MR. HARE:** *(Struggling up from the ground, he shouts out.)*
18   **I let him win!** *(MR. HARE collapses again as MR.*
19   *TORTOISE waves to the cameras victoriously. Curtain.)*
20
21
22 **Reference – Aesop's Fable**
23 "The Tortoise and the Hare"

20. You Lookin' at Me?

Cast of Characters:

LITTLE RED, the self-confident instructor and founder of Little Red's Self-Defense for the Unassertive.

SNOW WHITE, a sweet but naïve member of the class.

AURORA, a beauty who is prone to sleeping a lot.

CINDERELLA, a shy young lady from a broken home.

STUDENTS, others attending the class to build their confidence.

Props: None.

Scene:

The classroom of Little Red's Self-Defense for the Unassertive.

1   *(As the scene begins, there are several STUDENTS sitting*
2   *on the floor waiting for the class to begin. They are all*
3   *excited and nervous. Among them are SNOW WHITE,*
4   *AURORA, and CINDERELLA. LITTLE RED walks*
5   *confidently into the classroom, stands before the*
6   *students, and bows deeply.)*
7   **LITTLE RED: Good morning, students. I am your instructor**
8   **and the founder of Little Red's Self-Defense for the**
9   **Unassertive. Welcome. You have taken a huge step by**
10   **coming here today. From this moment on, your life will**
11   **be changed. By the end of this class, you will no longer**
12   **be living as sniveling little cowards. You will find your**
13   **true strength deep within you. The strength that will**
14   **propel you effortlessly to a higher state of being. The**
15   **strength that will enable you to become all that you are**
16   **meant to be.** *(The STUDENTS react with excitement and*
17   *enthusiasm. LITTLE RED paces slowly as she explains*
18   *further.)* **I know who you are. Oh, yes, I know very well**
19   **who you are! You are all naïve little cowards!** *(With*

1   *distaste)* **You were brought up to be sweet and kind**
2   **and gentle little ladies.** *(Strongly)* **And where has that**
3   **sweetness gotten you? Huh? You're vulnerable and**
4   **scared of your own shadows! I know it's true, because**
5   **I was once just like you! I used to skip through the**
6   **forest without a care in the world, happily visiting**
7   **the sick and infirmed, delivering muffins and cakes**
8   **to shut-ins and the less fortunate. I was just trying to**
9   **make the world a better place. Just like you are. Is**
10   **that such a terrible thing?** *(The STUDENTS react with*
11   *understanding. They have all been in the same*
12   *situation LITTLE RED is describing.)* **Well, I've got**
13   **news for you, ladies. Skipping through the world is**
14   **not as safe as it used to be, and there's no one out**
15   **there watching over you every minute. No, siree!**
16   **When you are out in the world, you are on your own!**
17   **It's up to you to keep yourself safe, or something**
18   **terrible could happen to you. You might even get**
19   **gobbled up by an ugly, vicious wolf!** *(The STUDENTS*
20   *gasp in horror.)* **That's right. That's what happened to**
21   **me. I was the picture of innocence until that fateful**
22   **day. If it hadn't been for that hunter wandering by, I**
23   **wouldn't be standing before you today. And I decided,**
24   **as I climbed out of that wolf's gut, never again! Never**
25   **again would I be victimized by the world!** *(The*
26   *STUDENTS are moved and applaud enthusiastically.)*
27   **And now, it's your turn. I am going to teach you all**
28   **how to take care of yourselves in this cruel,**
29   **dangerous world. Are you with me?**
30 **STUDENTS:** *(Together)* **We're with you!**
31 **LITTLE RED: That's what I like to hear! Now, I need my**
32   **first volunteer.**
33 **SNOW WHITE:** *(Waves her hand with vigor.)* **Oh, me! Me!**
34 **LITTLE RED: All right, young lady. You're up!** *(SNOW*
35   *WHITE jumps up and stands next to LITTLE RED.)*

1   **LITTLE RED: And what is your name?**

2   **SNOW WHITE: My name is Snow White, and I'm so**

3   **excited to be here. Yeah!**

4   **LITTLE RED: Very good, Snow White.** *(Casually)* **I just**

5   **want to present a little scenario to see how you would**

6   **react.**

7   **SNOW WHITE:** *(Giggling)* **OK. That sounds like fun!**

8   **LITTLE RED: Well, we'll see about that, won't we? Now,**

9   **Snow White – if that is your real name – suppose you**

10   **are quietly enjoying an afternoon in the woods,**

11   **minding your own business, not hurting a soul.**

12   **You're just doing a little light housework and**

13   **enjoying the little birds and wildlife, not a care in the**

14   **world, when suddenly, an evil-looking witch appears**

15   **dressed as a sweet little old lady. She offers you a**

16   **beautiful, ruby-red apple to eat, and you are so**

17   **hungry. What would you do?** *(LITTLE RED holds out*

18   *her hand to SNOW WHITE, as if it contains the apple.*

19   *SNOW WHITE is immediately transfixed on the*

20   *imaginary fruit. She starts to lick her lips in*

21   *anticipation. She slowly reaches out to take the*

22   *imaginary apple from LITTLE RED's hand. LITTLE*

23   *RED jerks her hand away.)* **What do you think you're**

24   **doing?**

25   **SNOW WHITE:** *(Coming to her senses)* **Well, I was just**

26   **going to accept the beautiful, juicy red apple and**

27   **take a bite. I'm so hungry.**

28   **LITTLE RED:** *(Emphatically)* **Not on your life! Do you**

29   **actually think an evil witch would be walking**

30   **through the woods, giving apples to strangers out of**

31   **the goodness of her heart?**

32   **SNOW WHITE: Well, I just thought ...**

33   **LITTLE RED:** *(Reprimanding her)* **You just thought! You**

34   **just thought! That kind of naïve thinking will get you**

35   **into deep doo-doo, lady!**

1   SNOW WHITE: So, what was I suppose to do?
2   LITTLE RED: Here, you hold out the apple, and I'll show
3   you what to do. *(SNOW WHITE holds out the imaginary*
4   *apple. LITTLE RED acts surprised. In a sweet little*
5   *"Snow White" voice)* Oh! An apple, for me? How sweet!
6   What a kind, generous old lady you are. *(LITTLE*
7   *RED's composure and voice changes completely.)*
8   Here's what I think of your perfect little apple!
9   *(LITTLE RED does a series of self-defense karate-type*
10   *chops toward the apple in SNOW WHITE's hand,*
11   *sending it flying through the air.)* Hai-ya! Hai-ya! Take
12   that! And take that! *(Ends with a defiant kick.)* Hai-ya!
13   *(The STUDENTS gasp in amazement and start to cheer.*
14   *LITTLE RED turns to SNOW WHITE.)* Now, you try.
15 SNOW WHITE: All right. I'll try. *(Gets herself ready and*
16   *then tries to imitate LITTLE RED's defensive moves. A*
17   *new spirit of assertiveness comes over her.)* You trying
18   to poison me, you old witch? You trying to poison me?
19   Well, take that! Hai-ya! *(Chops at the air.)* Hai-ya!
20   *(Chops at the air again.)* Take that! *(Does a fancy kick.)*
21   And take that! I don't want your stinking old apple!
22   Hai-ya! *(Triumphantly)* I don't eat between meals! So
23   there! *(The STUDENTS cheer. Now feeling strong and*
24   *fearless, SNOW WHITE takes a bow and happily sits*
25   *down. LITTLE RED is applauding for her, too.)*
26 LITTLE RED: Excellent work! Excellent! All right, who's
27   next? *(The STUDENTS raise their hands*
28   *enthusiastically. LITTLE RED chooses her next subject.*
29   *She points to AURORA.)* All right, you! Come on up
30   here. *(AURORA stands up and takes her place next to*
31   *LITTLE RED.)* And what is your name?
32 AURORA: *(Smiling sweetly)* My name is Aurora. *(Yawns a*
33   *huge yawn.)* Excuse me!
34 LITTLE RED: Are we keeping you up?
35 AURORA: Oh, no. I just always seem to be sleepy.

1   **LITTLE RED: Well, see if you can stay on your toes for this**
2   **scenario.** *(Starts to paint a word picture for AURORA.)*
3   **You're alone in a dark, drafty castle, when suddenly,**
4   **a strange-looking figure stands before you and starts**
5   **to hypnotize you.** *(Waves her hands in front of*
6   *AURORA as if to hypnotize her.)* **What do you do?**
7   **AURORA:** *(Considers this but is stumped.)* **Hmmmm. I fall**
8   **into a deep sleep that lasts for hundreds of years?**
9   **LITTLE RED: No, no, no! That is exactly what you don't do!**
10   **Absolutely** *no sleeping!* **That goes for everyone! Once**
11   **you fall asleep, you're completely out of control of**
12   **your own destiny. No! You turn to the dark figure,**
13   **point your finger at her, and say strongly, "You**
14   **lookin' at me?** *You lookin' at me?!"* **Then you hai-ya!**
15   *(Makes a chopping motion toward the dark figure.)* **And**
16   **you hai-ya!** *(Chops again with her other hand.)* **Then**
17   **you kick! Hai-ya!** *(Kicks a mighty blow toward the dark*
18   *figure.)* **Then you never have to be frightened again.**
19   **AURORA: Oh, dear. I don't know if I could do that.**
20   **LITTLE RED: You've got to dig deep. You've got to try to**
21   **find that inner strength that has eluded you for so**
22   **long.** *(Starts to wave her fingers in front of AURORA*
23   *again as if to hypnotize her.)*
24   **AURORA:** *(Gaining strength, she looks at LITTLE RED and*
25   *squints her eyes.)* **You tryin' to hypnotize me?** *You*
26   *tryin' to hypnotize me?* **Well, you just better back off**
27   **or I'll hai-ya!** *(Chops at the air in front of her.)* **And I'll**
28   **hai-ya!** *(Chops with the other hand.)* **And wait — here's**
29   **one more for good measure!** *(Kicks wildly.)* **Hai-ya!**
30   *(The STUDENTS applaud enthusiastically.)*
31   **LITTLE RED: I think you finally have the right idea. Next!**
32   *(The STUDENTS wave their hands in the air*
33   *enthusiastically. LITTLE RED calls on her last victim —*
34   *CINDERELLA.)* **You! You're up next.** *(CINDERELLA*
35   *takes the stage next to LITTLE RED. She waves to the*

1   *other students and smiles at them sweetly.)* **What's your**
2   **name, little lady?**
3 **CINDERELLA: My name is Cinderella.**
4 **LITTLE RED: Really? Cinderella? You students have the**
5   **strangest names. All right, Cinderella, here is your**
6   **situation. You come from a broken home. Your**
7   **father's remarried and doesn't give you the time of**
8   **day. Your stepmother is like someone out of a horror**
9   **film. She treats you terribly! She makes you scrub the**
10   **floors and do the laundry. You cook the meals, feed**
11   **the chickens, and sleep in a dank, dark little attic. You**
12   **are nothing more than a servant in your own home!**
13   *(CINDERELLA is starting to tear up. LITTLE RED gets*
14   *close to CINDERELLA's face.)* **Are you going to put up**
15   **with that kind of treatment?** *(CINDERELLA silently*
16   *nods "yes." LITTLE RED looks into her eyes and slowly*
17   *nods "no." CINDERELLA's head changes directions as*
18   *she nods "no" with LITTLE RED.)* **No, you don't put up**
19   **with it.**
20 **CINDERELLA:** *(Weakly)* **No, I don't put up with it.**
21 **LITTLE RED: Say it louder.**
22 **CINDERELLA:** *(Louder)* **No, I don't put up with it!**
23 **LITTLE RED: One more time with conviction!**
24 **CINDERELLA:** *(Even louder)* **No, I will not put up with it!**
25 **LITTLE RED:** *(Broadly)* **Now, what are you going to do**
26   **about it?**
27 **CINDERELLA:** *(Gaining strength)* **What am I going to do**
28   **about it? You want to know what I'm going to do**
29   **about it? I'm going to point to her and say,**
30   **"Stepmother, are you lookin' at me?** *Are you lookin' at*
31   *me?"* **Hai-ya!** *(Makes a chopping motion in the air.)* **Hai-**
32   **ya!** *(Chops again.)* **Hai-ya! Hai-ya!** *(Kicks in the air with*
33   *gusto.)* **That's what I'm going to do about it!** *(The*
34   *STUDENTS erupt in cheering and jump to their feet.)*
35 **LITTLE RED:** *(Looks around proudly.)* **Ladies, my work**

1   **here is done. Class dismissed!** *(Curtain)*
2
3
4   **References – Fairy Tales:**
5   The Story of "Little Red Riding Hood"
6   The Story of "Snow White and the Seven Dwarfs"
7   The Story of "Sleeping Beauty"
8   The Story of "Cinderella"

About the Author

Jan Peterson Ewen has been a professional singer, actor, and director for over thirty years. She has served as Founder and Artistic Director for Western Washington Center for the Arts in Port Orchard, Washington for the past eleven years, directing over sixty musicals and plays. She has developed musical theatre workshops for kids that have seen hundreds of children thrive and develop by learning the theatrical process.

Jan loves working with singers and actors of all ages and particularly has a heart for those who long to sing and act but lack the confidence to discover their talents. In order to reach as many students as possible, she has expanded her teaching to include a website called SING-NATURALLY.com which focuses on encouraging and developing fledgling singers and performers.

Jan lives in the beautiful Pacific Northwest with her talented musician husband, Bruce Ewen. She has three adult children, Peter, Rebecca, and Rachel, whose love of music and theater brings her immense joy. This is the third book of scenes Jan has published. The first two collections were published by Lillenas Publishing Company. For more information on the author and available resources, visit www.JanPetersonEwen.com.

Order Form

Meriwether Publishing Ltd.
PO Box 7710
Colorado Springs, CO 80933-7710
Phone: 800-937-5297 Fax: 719-594-9916
Website: www.meriwether.com

Please send me the following books:

_____ **Fractured Fairy Tales for Student Actors** $17.95
#BK-B354
by Jan Peterson Ewen
A collection of contemporary fairy tale scenes

_____ **Sixty Comedy Duet Scenes for Teens** $17.95
#BK-B302
by Laurie Allen
Real-life situations for laughter

_____ **Thirty Short Comedy Plays for Teens** $17.95
#BK-B292
by Laurie Allen
Plays for a variety of cast sizes

_____ **Make It Mystery #BK-B287** $19.95
by Craig Sodaro
An anthology of short mystery plays

_____ **62 Comedy Duet Scenes for Teens** $17.95
#BK-B332
by Laurie Allen
More real-life situations for laughter

_____ **Comedy Plays and Scenes** $17.95
for Student Actors #BK-B320
by Laurie Allen
Short sketches for young performers

_____ **Improv Ideas #BK-B283** $24.95
by Justine Jones and Mary Ann Kelley
A book of games and lists

These and other fine Meriwether Publishing books are available at
your local bookstore or direct from the publisher. Prices subject to
change without notice. Check our website or call for current prices.

Name: _____ email:_____

Organization name: _____

Address: _____

City: _____ State: _____

Zip: _____ Phone: _____

❏ **Check enclosed**

❏ **Visa / MasterCard / Discover / Am. Express #** _____

Signature: _____ *Expiration date:* _____ / _____ *CVV code:* _____
(required for credit card orders)

Colorado residents: Please add 3% sales tax.
Shipping: Include $3.95 for the first book and 75¢ for each additional book ordered.

❏ *Please send me a copy of your complete catalog of books and plays.*

Order Form

Meriwether Publishing Ltd.
PO Box 7710
Colorado Springs, CO 80933-7710
Phone: 800-937-5297 Fax: 719-594-9916
Website: www.meriwether.com

Please send me the following books:

_____ **Fractured Fairy Tales for Student Actors** $17.95
#BK-B354
by Jan Peterson Ewen
A collection of contemporary fairy tale scenes

_____ **Sixty Comedy Duet Scenes for Teens** $17.95
#BK-B302
by Laurie Allen
Real-life situations for laughter

_____ **Thirty Short Comedy Plays for Teens** $17.95
#BK-B292
by Laurie Allen
Plays for a variety of cast sizes

_____ **Make It Mystery #BK-B287** $19.95
by Craig Sodaro
An anthology of short mystery plays

_____ **62 Comedy Duet Scenes for Teens** $17.95
#BK-B332
by Laurie Allen
More real-life situations for laughter

_____ **Comedy Plays and Scenes** $17.95
for Student Actors #BK-B320
by Laurie Allen
Short sketches for young performers

_____ **Improv Ideas #BK-B283** $24.95
by Justine Jones and Mary Ann Kelley
A book of games and lists

**These and other fine Meriwether Publishing books are available at
your local bookstore or direct from the publisher. Prices subject to
change without notice. Check our website or call for current prices.**

Name: _____ email:_____

Organization name: _____

Address: _____

City: _____ State: _____

Zip: _____ Phone: _____

❏ **Check enclosed**

❏ **Visa / MasterCard / Discover / Am. Express #** _____

Signature: _____
(required for credit card orders)

Expiration
date: _____ / _____

CVV
code: _____

Colorado residents: Please add 3% sales tax.
Shipping: Include $3.95 for the first book and 75¢ for each additional book ordered.

❏ *Please send me a copy of your complete catalog of books and plays.*